Interior Design Atlas

KÖNEMANN

Project Management: Arco Editorial, S.A., Barcelona, Spain

Author: Francisco Asensio Cerver

Editor: Paco Asensio

Design: Mireia Casanovas Soley

Layout: Ricardo Alvarez, Jaume Martínez Coscojuela, Emma Termes Parera

Language Editing: Xavier Agramunt, Anna Tiessler

Photography: (c) Carme Macià, (c) Wayne Chazan, (c) Eugeni Pons, (c) Pere Planells, (c) Lluis Sans, (c) Jordi Sarrà, (c) David Cardelús, (c) Dennis Krukowski: p.14 (top left, small photo) Mark Zeff Consulting Group Inc., N.Y., USA; p.20 Nancy Mannuncci Inc., A.S.I.D., N.Y., USA; p.21 (top right) Jean P. Simmers Ltd., Rye, N.Y., USA; p.24 (bottom left) Rolf P. Seckinger; p.25 Luis Molina; p.274 (top left) Brenda Speight Frederiksburg, Texas, USA; p.274 (central left) Florence Perchuk, C.K.D., N.Y., USA; p.274 (bottom left) The Wetzel's Alexander Valey Vineyards, Healsburg, California, USA; p.275 The Teddy Roosevelt House Sagamore Hill, Oyster Bay, N.Y., USA; p.276 (top left) Florence Perchuk, C.K.D., N.Y., USA; p.357 (top left) Philadelphia Entrance Hall; p.358 (top left) Iron Horse Vineyard Sanoma County, California, USA; p.358 (bottom left) Jeanne-Aelia-Desparment-Hart, N.Y. 10019; p.417 Paul Silverman; p.422 Yancy Hughes, Alabama, USA; p.431 Healing Barsanti Inc., N.Y., USA; p.475 Mariette Himes Gomez Assoc. Inc., N.Y., USA; p.487 Kuehner Family, Pennsylvania, USA; p.512 David Webster & Assoc., N.Y., USA; p.616 Architect Jaime Aldama, Guadalajara Jalisco, MÈxico; p.618 John Rodgers, Southampton, Long Island, USA; p.623 Robert DeCarlo, N.Y., USA; p.624 Anthony Childs Inc., Washington D.C., USA; p.661 (bottom left) Robert L. Zion Landscape Design, Monmouth County, N.J., USA; p.690 (bottom left) Michael Formica Inc., N.Y., USA; p.692 Halsted Wells & Assoc., N.Y., USA; p.263 (top right) Robert L. Zion Landscape Design, Monmouth County, N.J., USA; p.693 (bottom right) Burgess Lea, Pennsylvania's Buck County, USA; p.694 (top left) David Webster & Assoc., N.Y., USA; p.694 (bottom left) David Webster & Assoc., N.Y., USA; p.695 Michael Formica Inc., N.Y., USA; p.734 (bottom left) Birch Coffey Design Assoc., N.Y., USA; p.734 (bottom left) Virgian Witbeck, N.Y., USA; p.775 Rofl P. Seckinger; p.776 Mark Zef Consulting Group Inc., N.Y., USA; p.777 (top right) Peter F. Carlson & Assoc. L.L.C., Lyme, Connecticut, USA; p.778 (bottom left) Peter F. Carlson & Assoc. L.L.C., Lyme, Connecticut, USA.

Original title: Decoratión del hogar y mueble moderno

Translation from Spanish: G. Bickford, M. McMeekin, M. Reece and S. Wiles in association with First Edition Translations

English Language Editing: Kay Hyman in association with First Edition Translations

Typesetting: The Write Idea in association with First Edition Translations

Project Management: Beatrice Hunt for First Edition Translations, Cambridge, UK

Project Coordination: Nadja Bremse

Cover Design: Peter Feierabend, Claudio Martinez

Production: Ursula Schümer

Printing and Binding: Poligrafiche Bolis S.p.A. , Azzano S. Paolo

Printed in Italy
ISBN 3-8290-3563-2

10 9 8 7 6 5 4 3 2 1

Introduction

Our home is an intimate and personal space, but the rhythm of our lives does not allow us to enjoy it as much as we would like. Naturally, everybody likes their home to be cozy and comfortable, a space with which we can identify and where we feel completely at ease.

It is obvious that the choice of furnishings for our home must have a practical aspect, and the ideal choice finds a balance between function and style. There are many different decorative styles, and none is more appropriate than any other. It is best not to become obsessed with one specific approach. Although the decoration of our house demands coherence and the avoidance of clashing contrasts, a degree of eclecticism is also interesting. The mixing of certain materials produces very good results, so that if we like wood, for example, we can combine it with steel. We don't have to opt for a totally rustic look. With a little common sense, each person's needs and taste will dictate the design of his or her home. Fashion must never be the sole criterion.

Every designer champions different approaches to the planning of interiors. Some emphasize color, imagination, and creativity. Other professionals are drawn to breezy designs which create bright, cheerful, and relaxed spaces, whilst others are more conservative and prefer simple, refined, and subdued interiors. However, what all designers have in common is the constant search for furniture and environments that enhance our quality of life.

These days it is not only wealthy people who seek to decorate their home. With a little good taste and imagination we can all design beautiful spaces. Moreover, there are shops that offer designer furniture at fairly accessible prices, although, of course, a larger budget can provide access to furniture and fittings from the most prestigious designers, as well as the services of an interior designer.

Until recently, the interior designer did not exist, and it was left to furniture salesmen and upholsterers, among others, to give advice about decoration. At the height of the twentieth century, the job of the interior designer came into being, although it was initially linked to the antiques trade. Today, the existence of courses in interior architecture vouches for the interest that this subject has created and the status that the profession has acquired.

The decoration of a space involves many elements. It is not just a question of furniture. Color and lighting as well as wall and floor coverings also come into play. When we create a specific environment and choose its components, we must also take into account the budget, the space available, the age of the building, and the number of people living in the home and their ages.

A house's finishing touches undoubtedly lie in the decorative details: works of art, such as sculptures and paintings, lamps and plants. In every case, the distribution of each room must be decided thoughtfully and methodically. If necessary, make a scale plan of the room with all its elements and combine them until you find the most satisfactory layout.

It is difficult to create a pure line to run through our home. We can achieve an equally harmonious effect by mixing various styles. In the 1970s the High Tech style burst on the scene, conceiving space as a functional working environment. Interior design used industrial materials such as glass, metal, plastic, and rubber, but perhaps its most innovative trait was the recycling of industrial objects for the home. In fact, High Tech proved not to be a passing fashion but became the basis for a more contemporary trend: the technological style. It is clear that this is a reaction against the rustic style, just as High Tech had rejected the idea of a home as a comfortable refuge but saw it as a space full of surprises, resulting from the combination of unusual elements.

If you want a space free of useless objects and any decorative excess, you will probably feel at home with the technological style. Pure lines and simplicity reign supreme; typical materials are chromed steel and black leather. The furnishings are timeless and their discretion means that they do not become boring. They are complemented by walls in white or gray, never bright colors. The idea is to integrate the walls, floors, and furniture. It is a style that permits a degree of flexibility but requires great compositional coherence.

On the other hand, many people dream of a rustic style for their home. They love old furniture and antiques, and want to turn their home into a space where warmth and natural materials, especially wood, take pride of place. The advantage of the rustic style is that it permits decorative touches that give a home a trendy and welcoming feel. We can create a rustic style abounding in freshness, creativity, and modernity. For example, rustic houses often leave the old stone of the walls exposed, and an extraordinarily innovative effect can be obtained by painting the other walls in blue or terracotta tones. This results in a warm and trendy home. The rustic style is not incompatible with functionality, although it does require more decorative details than the technological style. Its spirit is not as practical. The rustic style can be counterbalanced by avant-garde fittings, such as lamps, or by the colors and patterns on the wall, by pictures, flowers, couches, curtains, and other textile complements.

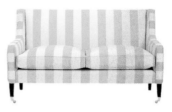

The classic style is essentially urban and mixes one-off pieces with avant-garde elements. It is modern and highly refined, but avoids any stridency or surprises. It seeks to create a welcoming environment by fusing classic and contemporary esthetics — not always an easy task. It is always advisable to maintain a feeling of spaciousness. In the classic style, plants, pictures, sculptures, carefully chosen decorative objects and a profusion of prints are crucial in giving homes those highly esteemed touches of refinement. If you prefer beauty to be expressed in minimal terms, this is not the style for you as it is just the opposite of minimalism. Attaining a satisfactory classic style requires a long process, as it is not easy to find one-off antique pieces that fit in perfectly. A pleasing overall effect is not enough; with this style you must pay close attention to every detail.

As in the case of High Tech, Postmodernism grew out of architecture — as a reaction to the formal simplicity advocated by High Tech. At the end of the twentieth century, the Postmodernist style still has a lot to say. It turns its back on simplicity, excessive order, and rationalism; and it also stays clear of black and white. It constitutes an explosion of colors: green, blue, yellow, and red mingle uninhibitedly to create an innovative avant-garde space. It does not require excessive furnishing but does demand a greater

attention to forms and details than the technological style. It combines the most diverse styles, and it allows every individual to express his or her sense of beauty and harmony. There are no rules: it is a relaxed style with no signs of inflexibility. As it is a very daring style, there is a risk that it gets boring more quickly than a more subdued decoration.

Many people are not entirely satisfied with the rustic, classic, technological, or Postmodernist styles, but borrow ideas from all of them to create a personalized whole that satisfies their specific requirements. This critical spirit is undoubtedly positive. We must be conscious of the advantages and inconveniences of each style. A degree of eclecticism is possible, and is particularly popular with young people, who are usually on a limited budget. The aim is to create a beautiful environment using a variety of informal but functional furnishings. A very modern style may be chosen for a particular room, but one corner can be decorated with very inexpensive but attractive rustic elements.

However, notwithstanding this stylistic freedom, certain rules must be taken into account in decoration, if only to break them. Ultimately, decoration is the task of a lifetime, and the most interesting and enjoyable part is to see how a home evolves over the years.

Halls and corridors

An attractive hall will win us over as soon as we enter a house. The hall is the prelude to the home and, as such, we must take care of its style. It is where we receive visitors, even the most unwelcome ones that will not go any further. For our guests, however, it will be a transition stage, and even though it may only be a passageway, it is very pleasant — even for the occupants of the house — to receive a good impression every time the front door is opened.

The size of the house and the hall itself will determine the latter's function and decoration. If the space in the home is limited, the hall must convey a feeling of expansiveness, so we should not overburden it with unnecessary objects. White is the ideal color for the walls, and we should not hang too many pictures on them. Furthermore, a single piece of furniture will be more effective than many decorative objects.

However, if our home is so small that we need to use the hall as an extra room, we must store things in an orderly manner, otherwise it will end up becoming a lumber room. Instead, we can put in a closet covering an entire wall, to serve as a storage space for shoes, videotapes, suitcases, coats, or other objects. In any case, if we need to use the hall space, it is important to do so as discreetly as possible, so that it does not become overwhelming.

Even if a hall is particularly large, it is not advisable to overload it with objects and furniture. Beauty usually lies in simplicity, spaciousness, and luminosity. We can permit ourselves the luxury of decorating it with some details that will charm both visitors and owners. For example, if we put in a desk, a table lamp, and a chair, we can improvise an elegant office. Some floral details are also suitable.

The floor of a hall is often badly treated. On rainy days we come in with wet shoes, and children sometimes have their footwear covered in mud. It is therefore important to choose a floor that is resistant as well as decorative. In any case, we must not forget what type of flooring we have installed in the rest of the home. That way we can avoid any undesirable contrast in style that will make a break in continuity.

Corridors are another kind of passageway. We do not spend much time in them, but that does not mean that we must neglect their decoration. A beautiful house requires care in every nook and cranny. If our budget does not allow us to spend very much on the corridor, we must just make sure that it is elegant and luminous. There is nothing more unsettling than a gloomy corridor, reminiscent of a dark tunnel.

One very modern and fanciful option is to paint "*trompe-l'œils*" on the walls, not to create huge landscapes, but to add small details.

"*Trompe-l'œils*" are suitable for doors, fireplaces, furniture, and screens, as well as being an original way of dressing corridor walls. However, the most common means of decorating corridors is by hanging pictures on their walls. Family photos, hung like portraits, also produce very good results. Note that the effect is not very pleasing if the pictures are placed without any planning, for instance without any space between them. As always, restraint and good distribution are decisive factors.

If we should want to make a corridor functional, we have several possibilities. We can install a big closet along one side, or put furniture with shelves in its corners, or take advantage of the ceiling by fitting a loft.

However, the crucial element in a corridor, whether we opt for a decorative model or a more functional one, is to illuminate it intensely. Normally it is deprived of sunlight, and so we have to endow it with artificial light. A corridor with wonderful pictures is worthless if we plunge into murky light when we enter it.

Once again, pale-colored walls will help redistribute the light better. The ideal solutions are halogen lamps fitted into the ceiling, or designer wall lamps. If this general lighting does not permit a full appreciation of the paintings or other decorative objects, we can opt for spotlights that pick them out individually.

First impressions

The first impression always counts and the hall is the place where it starts to be formed. The hall also serves as a connection to more personal and finished interiors. The details on display there constitute a small showcase for the personality of the home.

The hall becomes a reflection of a house's character by incorporating details of the styles on display in the various interiors.

A couple of books and a few well chosen details provide hints of the personality of the home.

An original and entertaining idea, with a theater seat combined with a percussion instrument within the same chromatic range. The ensemble announces an interest in the stage as a theme of the decoration.

Classic furniture in an interior packed with details and subtlety. The visual strength of these elements erases the impression that the hall is just for transit.

This hall has been decorated in an updated version of the classic style. The mirror reinforces the sense of space, and also serves a practical purpose – we can check our appearance before going out.

Simple lines in a classic hall, containing only a matching table and chair and a white cabinet displaying English crockery.

A staircase in the hall

For practical reasons, the staircase in many houses starts in the hall, thus automatically converting it into a crossroads leading to different parts of the home. The distinctive nature of each space is preserved by transforming the hall and staircase into a single area of transit between the different rooms and their respective decorative styles.

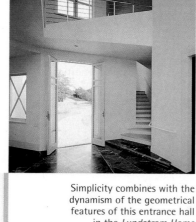

Simplicity combines with the dynamism of the geometrical features of this entrance hall in the *Lundstrom Home* designed by David Connor.

Hall with very vivid and cheerful details. The entrance to the house is situated between two floors, and so this area serves as both a hall and a connecting passageway.

Simplicity of finish for this combination, realized in the *Casa Amat* by Antoni de Moragues. The monochrome effect produced by the combination of wood and the cream color of the wall increases the impression of a transit area leading to more personal spaces.

Classic hall with an English-style staircase. The space is designed to lead on to four areas of the house that are sufficiently independent not to require any direct communication between each other. Normally, this type of layout is found on the upper floor, where bathrooms and bedrooms are, neatly closing off and separating the most private part of the house.

The staircase forms an opening behind the front door that forms an integral part of this entrance. The staircase's romantic balustrade strives for a touch of originality by replacing the traditional banisters with a simple rope.

Absolute simplicity for this hall, which updates a rustic style.

Simplicity in passing

A simple piece of side furniture or an easy chair and mirror are sufficient to decorate a hall, endowing it with a sober well-balanced image of functional austerity.

This structure, combining wood and glass in simple forms and straight lines, aims for coordination with the painting that dominates the space.

Absolute simplicity of line in an ensemble with a ledge and mirror. The curved shape of the shelf entices the visitors to move on into the interior.

Colzani is responsible for *Garden*, a design carried out in solid cherrywood. Combining dried flowers and garden elements, its finishing suggests the change in atmosphere that is experienced on entering or leaving the house.

With a classic structure and the architecture of a rural house, this ensemble creates a sober yet luxurious setting, thanks to the size of the space available for a simple transit area.

A plain shelf provides the structure for this setting, which combines simple solutions with details such as the three drawers hanging from the central level.

Opposite: A unit by Porada, set against the wall, emphasizing the curved shapes of the hall. The element's only straight line is its meeting point with the wall, providing a contrast between the linearity of the two-dimensional features and the curves of the solid forms.

Impressive entrances

The idea of the hall as an indispensable practical element in a house has lost ground in recent years. It was previously considered a functional room that could also have a great visual impact. Nowadays, the area given over to this space has been considerably reduced in the modern home.

The generous dimensions of this entrance mean that furniture can be dispensed with altogether. A large hall benefits from the visual effect of the space itself, and does not require any furniture.

The rug is the element that subtly marks out this space. This idea is suitable for halls that need to define their space more clearly because of their large size.

The classic structure of this hall permits the inclusion of a *trompe-l'œil*.

The structure of this rustic-style hall is dominated by a series of arches, which bestow great character on the setting.

White is the undisputed star in this surprising space. The original addition of a metal grille, and the definition of the room's limits with a drape, both add interest to the setting.

Laura Ashley presents this English-style ensemble. The warmth of the wood, the pale colors, and the decorative details in all the corners give this hall a distinctive personality.

Ideas from modern architecture

Halls that lead into modern architectural interiors, with rational forms and continuous lines, are built on the basis of spatial simplicity. They are large spaces with a minimum of elements, which allow the architecture itself to be the main feature of the interior design and decoration.

The layouts of many homes today, in which space is at a premium, have given rise to distributive solutions like this one from the Calligaris company.

Detail from *Babà*, the hybrid of bench and hall furnishing proposed by Calligaris.

Luminosity is another of the characteristics of these spaces. The few decorative elements in this hall are silhouetted by the intense light, thus acquiring a fragile and ethereal quality.

The utter simplicity of the hall in the *Insignia House* seeks to entice the visitor to move on into the interior.

Detail of the hall in the *Insignia House*. The semicircular form that encloses a side space provides the link between the hall and the corridor.

The modern layout of this hall in the *Casa Bergadà* contrasts with the classic structure of the dome in the ceiling.

Furnishing the hall

It is difficult to find the right balance between functionality and esthetic considerations when choosing a piece of furniture for the hall. The lack of other furniture around it means that, sometimes with the aid of a mirror, it is responsible for the tone of the setting.
One of the most popular decorative solutions is the placement of objects and the use of small details to create a range of effects and illustrate the character of the house.

Punxi model from Porada. Its structural simplicity permits the presence of other decorative elements without overpowering the space. The glass semicircle, resting on a stylized, solid cherrywood base, combines elegance and discretion.

Hugonet center table, lacquered in white, with a perforated wooden top.

Classic piece made of dark walnut. This type of furniture has changed over the years, forsaking some of its decorative character and stylistic details to become eminently functional.

Porada is responsible for this unit, made up of a chest of drawers with casters and a tower with shelves and a mirror. The functionality of this piece and its simple but elegant design make it a perfect choice for halls that are restricted in size.

Romantic white hall by Laura Ashley. Stylistic details, such as the color combination of the handles and the top, give this piece of furniture a distinctive personality.

A classic piece of furniture with simple linear forms. The structure of this piece draws on the tradition of the wall table, very popular in period furniture.

Original halls

As an indicator of the character of a home, the hall can take on a distinctive personality, which can be appreciated at first sight, to herald a house imbued with originality and invention.

Cuccagna is a mountable pillar unit from the Porada company that is surprisingly versatile and attractive. Clearly modern in structure, in a combination of sand and wood tones, it fits in with all types of settings and styles.

The presence of a sink full of plants indicates a very individual exoticism.

A useful and attractive receptacle, in the form of a traditional milk churn painted in vivid colors. The originality of this element, named *Milk* by the Graepel company, makes it ideal as a cheerful detail in the corner of the hall.

The hall in *Bonatti House* is structured around an interplay of open and closed levels resulting from the distinctive layout of the walls and partitions, which allow part of the dining room to be seen from the entrance.

Detail of *Bonatti House*, showing the original decoration of the doors and walls. The arrows fulfill the dual function of indicating and decorating.

An interesting idea from Porada, in which two pieces of furniture are designed to be combined together. A bench and a small table can adapt their shapes to offer one original solution.

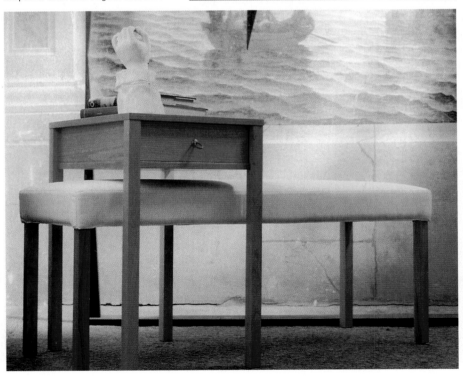

Wall elements

Lack of space in the hall gives rise to a group of elements which are placed on the wall, in order to take the maximum advantage of the space available.
Mirrors, shelves, and small fitted display cabinets give personality to a hall, without having to resort to large pieces of furniture.

The Xavier Pujol company is responsible for this combination of simple forms. The refined esthetic of the installation has a strong horizontal plane, which contrasts with the vertical line of the lamp.

Wall mirror with central band from the Porada company. The panel and shelf are made of cherrywood.

The importance of wall elements for the hall is enhanced by the addition of wall-lamps or pictures, which endow a space with personality.

A large circular mirror dominates the hall, which leads on to a corridor. Narrow spaces are the ideal setting for mirrors, as they provide light and create a deceptive feeling of spaciousness.

Miró is a wall mirror from the Porada company, acting as a canvas which reflects the interior of the house.

Modular combination for a hall from the Xavier Pujol company. The various elements are arranged to follow the plane of the wall, thus creating a highly versatile unit.

Living rooms

The living room is a space to be enjoyed, where the whole family gets together and guests are received. It has many roles, and so its furnishings should reflect a well planned and functional distribution. This room is used for reading, conversing, listening to music, watching television and resting. It is also, of course, a room in which objects are kept and put on display.

Consequently, we must provide it with comfortable chairs and containers for storing all kinds of things. Lighting is also fundamental, and the greatest care must be taken over the choice of the right lamp for the reading corner. The environmental lighting can be subdued, provided we combine it with specific spotlights for carrying out different activities.

Even if we have a fairly spacious living room, it is not appropriate to fill it up with furniture. Elegance lies in simplicity. A large relaxing space requires an economy of elements. Rarely used furniture should be replaced by other more functional and efficient pieces. If the room is small it is best not to opt for large couches, as we are seeking to create a space which is as uncluttered as possible. It is always an advantage to have individual armchairs, which are flexible as regards positioning, and light and easily movable furniture.

One interesting option is modular furniture. Modules, with their well defined and rational forms, dominated by straight lines, have the advantage of being spatially flexible and open to subsequent enlargements if we require them. Modules incorporate shelves, drawers, and display cabinets, and can therefore hold books, decorative objects, and a wide range of knickknacks. They can also contain audio-visual equipment.

Years ago, the whole family gathered round the fireplace; these days, the television is the focal point, although the fireplace still reigns with distinction in some privileged living rooms, giving them a welcoming touch. If we are not lucky enough to have a fireplace in the house, but

would still like to have such a feature, we can opt for gas stoves which imitate log and wood fires. They consume more fuel than traditional stoves, but, on the other hand, we can enjoy an apparently real fire without ever having to clean the grate.

Works of art comprise another eminently decorative element in the living room. We all like to hang pictures in the living room, because it is the appropriate place to enjoy them. However, we must decide on the esthetic effect we are trying to create. This is not a question of putting up paintings at random. We must hang them at the right height and, according to the work, either on their own or in a group with others. In some cases individual spotlights will be required to bring out the best in a painting.

Side tables are essential pieces of furniture in any living room. The variety of forms and sizes on offer means that they have a superb capacity for spatial adaptation. We can thus put them in front of the couch, to work on, or place them in the corners, or on either side of the couch, normally as a support for lamps. It is important not only to look for a good design but also to opt for quality. We can choose between a great variety of materials — wrought iron, stainless steel, wood, glass, marble — and styles — oriental, Arab, classical, sophisticated.

The other vital pieces of furniture in the living room are the couch and the armchairs. These represent the paradigm of relaxation and social life, as they accommodate our guests. It is best to choose very adaptable couches, with straight lines, deep seats, and high backrests. Comfort is of primary importance, but the durability of the upholstery must be taken into account. It can have smooth prints or a slightly textured surface; prints do not get so dirty as textures.

The decoration of the living room will also be subject to factors like cleaning and the age of the main features in the house.

Spaces filled with light

Until a few decades ago the living room was divided into small independent zones, each fulfilling a specific task. These days the trend is to unify space to attain a degree of versatility.

The combination of colors serves to define areas bathed in light. An explosion of tones – white, fuchsia, lilac and moss green – decorate this space, dominated by a large couch with sinuous forms. *Rosenthal House* by Frank Fitzgibbons.

A large living room has been put in on the first floor of the house overlooking the street, with a couch against the wall which is totally camouflaged and integrated into the overall setting. A simple eating area, leading onto the kitchen, creates contrasts of color. *O Residence* by Iida.

In the *Floral House* in London the architect Peter Romaniuk has created an enormous and unique space without any dividing partitions or screens, an environment similar to a loft.

Furniture with simple and slender forms for a room which gives pride of place to the transparent architecture of Wellington Quigley.

The pale pink tones of a house designed by Bosco Gutiérrez, which evokes traditional ethnic decoration, provide a framework for a large space with couches arranged in the form of a closed U. This option marks out a large area.

General view of the living room. A large module separates the kitchen and serves as a spatial reference point for the decoration of the rest of the room. *Price O'Reilly House*, the work of Engelee/Moore in Sydney, Australia.

The *Bielicky House* by Wolfgang Döring has given pride of place to paneled windows, which provide a setting for a living room with couches looking on to large open areas.

It is often possible to divide a well lit space into several multifunctional areas. The upper floor of the house has a small part given over to a back-up living room, with a designer armchair. *Psyche House* in the Netherlands, by René Van Zuuk.

Two couches forming an L shape on a parquet platform create a cozy space dominated by a spectacular red rug and a glass table. The living room is enclosed by structural elements, such as the columns. *Check House* in Singapore, the work of Teck Kiam Tan.

A couch placed against the wall frames an area dominated by a center table and a cotton rug. The two-seater couch is made of padded crushed velvet with sycamore finishing. The cushions are extremely durable. This model is by Roche & Bobois.

Conversation areas

The distribution of seating defines the area for meetings and conversations in a living room. The most common distributions are L or U shaped, or in parallel, although in the case of three-piece suites the natural distribution is still that of the armchairs separated from each other and facing the couch. L- and U-shaped compositions are practical with modular couches, particularly if they occupy the corners of the room. A parallel distribution, with two couches facing each other, is normally used when they occupy a central space, away from the walls. In any case, the provision of seats is increased by modular installations, and by other more informal seats, like poufs.

Couches placed in linear positions create bright and roomy spaces. The *Oberon* couch, designed by Lievore Asociados, has a wooden structure upholstered with polyurethane coating, with a protective textile cover, and the back and arms in air-fiber. The cushion covers can all be removed.

A discussion area centered around a modular couch can provide a host of combinations. These versatile models form corner compositions which are very useful for saving space. The couch in the photograph is the *Ocean* model designed by Swan, consisting of 20 different juxtaposed elements with a wooden structure and a practical metal support to enhance comfort. The covers can be taken off all the elements for cleaning.

Two couches forming an L shape leave room at the ends for a circular table and a rectangular one which gives the ensemble a finishing touch. *Prima Base* from Seat & Relax by Mobil Girgi is a modular couch with an innovative design in crushed velvet or leather.

A classical distribution consisting of a three-seater couch and an armchair made of wood supporting a shell of rigid expanded polyurethane. Model by Moroso, with covers which are completely removable and goose-feather filling.

A U-shaped composition with a practical rectangular table saves space in a large living room. *Lisbona* couch from Mobil Girgi in leather or crushed velvet with walnut or cherrywood.

Two armchairs can take the place of a couch in a discussion area. *B & B armchairs from Italy.*

A cotton rug is the decorative element which separates three-seater couches marked by their distinctive formal simplicity. Design by Adriano Piazzessi.

An aluminum bookcase is complemented by a modular couch in an irregular L shape, which stands out on account of its sinuous lines and forms. *Bench System* model by Piero Lissoni for Living Divano.

Couches at right angles, complemented by two small beech-wood tables.

Area dividers

The elements which separate areas in living rooms are essential to their spatial dynamics and unity. They can be of three types: permanent, either architectural or otherwise (columns or partitions); provisional and mobile, like screens; and those consisting of a well selected piece of furniture.

Two period chairs fix the discussion area and divide it from the rest of the living room.

A low wall defines the dining area and separates it from the rest of the space.

A staircase and glass-fronted bookcases isolate a relaxation area with a modern linear couch from the rest of the library.

A large white DM panel separates the two bulky armchairs from the rest of the house. A wooden staircase also defines the area.

A living room area is placed in the loft. A large conversation area has been set up to make full use of the space.

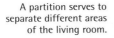

A wooden beam hanging from the wall is the center of attention of this living room with in-built couches.

A partition serves to separate different areas of the living room.

A sensually curved screen is very useful for separating different areas.

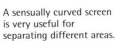

Wood in the living room

Wood appears in all living rooms as a dominating element, a connecting theme giving unity to the space. In the eclectic urban language of decoration, wood subjected to different industrial treatments appears with cherry and pine tones, or in exotic varieties such as nyatoh and bubinga.

Sofa with a wooden back and aluminum legs. *Jules et Jim* model designed by Enrico Franzolini for Moroso.

Modular bookcase with aluminum fittings and transparent glass panels. Designed by Interi.

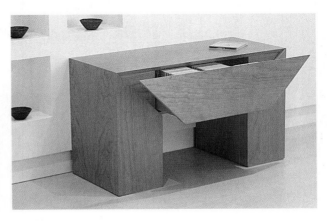

Table made of cherry wood and designed to store compact disks. The hidden runners of the drawers are telescopic and close automatically. It is manufactured in three tones with different finishes. *Peso* model, designed by L. Alba & J.M. Casaponsa and produced by Estudi Metro.

Armchair with sinuous armrests in beech. The table has a walnut finish. Produced by Interi.

Modular bookcase, stocked with books and objects, in natural wood. Design by Bessana.

Below and right: The parquet, the trimmings of the small center table, and the frame of the armchairs all demonstrate the importance of wood in modern settings. Armchairs designed by Stua.

Left: Small wooden cupboard in a cherry tone, with aluminum legs. Produced by Cassina.

Below: *Florence* is a set with an armchair and footrest with a wooden structure, upholstered in polyurethane and covered with protective fabric. Design by Lievore Asociados for Perobell.

Bip Hop unit with a cherry veneer and unified with solid beech. It has shelves in the center and on the sides. Design by Roche & Bobois.

Dama unit comprising wooden modules with metal handles. The doors are made of frosted glass. Produced by Galli.

Collection of table bases which, with the minimalist and entertaining design of their supports at several heights, and their metallic finishing, match the various types of tabletops on offer, appropriate for use in both the home and public spaces.

Versatile two-seaters

The two-seater couch is sufficiently flexible to be adapted to any space. It usually measures between 65 inches (165 cm) and 69 inches (175 cm) in length. The current model, in fashion since the 1960s, favors wide armrests with a fluffy filling and fabrics which resist stains and dirt.

Two-seater with removable covers and classic wooden feet. *Bristol* design by J. Casadesús for Cycsa.

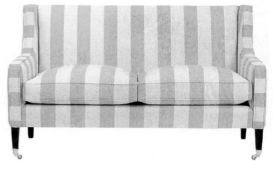

Couch with casters for greater mobility. The upholstery features a fabric with yellow and white stripes. *Santiago* model by Kilo Americano.

Two-seater couch in the classical style, with turned wooden legs. *Salamanca* model by Kilo Americano.

Two-seater couch with two-tone upholstery in gray and moss green. It has legs in glossy aluminum. Design by Hugo Ruiter for Leolux.

Frog is a two-seater couch designed by Piero Lissoni for Leolux, made with cotton cords or transparent PVC and an epoxy powdered coated tubular metal structure.

Two-seater with striking contrast between black and gray. *Zilia* design by A. Hieronimus for Leolux.

Colibri is an aerodynamic two-seater with a very practical little table attached. Design by Jan Armgardt.

Sinuous geometrical lines for a cream-colored avant-garde two-seater.

Balestro collection by *Living Divani.* Created with a broad ergonomic headrest by Piero Lissoni.

Asanti model by
Sancal in wood with
a reinforced core
and fluffy seats.

The *Denver* collection by
Cycsa has a wooden structure
with steel springs serving as
suspension for the seat.

Two-seater with wide armrests and side-flaps.
Design by Piero Lissoni for Living Divani.

Inflatable plastic
couch by Ikea.

Couch with loose feather cushions
to support the back. Beech legs
and washable covers. It is
designed by Erika Pekkari for Ikea.

Comfortable and long-lasting

Couches must be solid, deep, and made with their pressure points close together to ensure that they last. *Hello* series for Comfort, with an adjustable lamp and wooden side supports which serve as back-up tables.

Obviously the most striking features in a couch are its form and upholstery, but when you are buying one it is also essential to assess the quality of the structure, the support system, the various types of filling, and the upholstery technique.

Lucerna is designed by Emaf Progetti for Zanotta and has resistant aluminum legs and reinforcements in the backs and seats.

Paresse couch, created by H. Hopfer, on a solid beech structure assembled using dowels. From Roche & Bobois.

Highly resistant couch made with Emotion leather, with stitched and pleated trimming with matching thread, and suspension from spiral steel springs. *Farniente* model by Roche & Bobois.

Simple is a unit from Moroso made in wood covered with rigid expanded polyurethane. The cushions are stuffed with goose feathers.

Small bolsters and wide pillows make possible a siesta for two. It has seat cushions in triple-density foam and a framework made of beech. *Proprieté Privée* model from Roche & Bobois.

The *Novecento* line, designed by Antonio Citterio with a frame covered in rigid expanded polyurethane. It is produced by Moroso.

Waiting is a design by Rodolfo Dordoni for Moroso, of steel covered with rigid expanded polyurethane. The legs are made of aluminum, and their height can be adjusted.

Couch with reinforced aluminum frame which makes it specially longlasting and resistant to use. *Zurigo* design by Alfredo Häberlo and Christophe Marchand for Zanotta.

Lineal unit by Ximo Roca for Bonestil, in wood with textile latticework and reinforced sides. The upholstery is treated to make it stain resistant.

The couch family

The armchair is the natural complement to the couch. It is an article which has acquired great formal variety, and sound criteria and good taste are needed to purchase the appropriate model. Today's trends favor small armchairs, and even the "Art Deco" style of the 1920s and 1930s.

Moove armchair in leather with legs made of soldered steel tubing. To match it, a useful footrest. Design by Pascal Mourgue of Cassina.

Another version of *Moove* resembling a chaise longue, upholstered in red with all its covers removable for cleaning.

Opposite: Armchairs with an elegant and slender profile, made of beech-wood. Design by Giacomo Passal for Andreu World.

New York collection with 1950s-style lines. It is made with a wooden framework. The seat and back are made of polyurethane foam covered with polyester fiber. It is an elegant design by Cycsa.

Ergonomic armchair with all its covers removable. Nickel-plated steel legs with the outer part in natural wenge cherry or transparent plastic. *Malaparte* model from B & B Italia.

Opposite: Small armchair on casters, upholstered with cotton cover. *Do, Re, Mi* model, designed by Rodolfo Dordoni for Moroso.

Traditional *Chester* armchair, up-dated with modern fabrics and pale wood. Designed by Cycsa.

Cambridge armchair with a frame of solid beech and composite board covered with polyester foam. Varnished beech legs and removable covers. Model from Habitat.

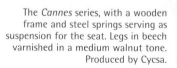

Florence is an armchair with a romantic air, with aluminum legs and incorporating a practical footrest. Model by B & B Italia.

The *Cannes* series, with a wooden frame and steel springs serving as suspension for the seat. Legs in beech varnished in a medium walnut tone. Produced by Cycsa.

Ateneu, designed by Massana-Tremoleda for Perobell, in wood covered with polyurethane and dacron.

Mantis armchair from Interi,
with wooden sidepieces.

Badajoz armchair, upholstered in
Vichy check, with turned legs.
Design by Kilo Americano.

The center table

This is the ideal piece of furniture for the meeting area and the center around which seats are distributed. These days it has become a favorite of designers, and there are many ingenious and original ideas, with drawers, modules, and folding tops.

Table with a beveled glass top, from Chueca.

This center table gives a duality of tones to the living room.

Square table in solid cherry with a frosted glass top. *Merlino* model, design by T. Colzani. From Porada.

Table in solid cherry with a transparent glass top fixed to its wooden structure. From Porada.

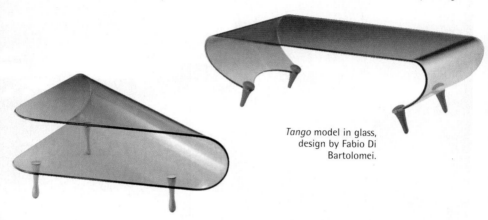

Opposite: In settings with large couches, it is advisable to have rectangular tables which run along some of the length of the couch. Table made of wood and transparent glass.

Tango model in glass, design by Fabio Di Bartolomei.

Today's center tables are bringing back the traditional forms of the 1970s. *Albatros* model, design by Roberto Semprini for Fiam Italia.

Small table made of a single piece of glass, without any joins or edges. It has an extra mobile element on casters which can be kept underneath. Design by Angelo Cortesi for Fiam Italia.

Pale-colored woods with a Nordic influence enhance center tables when combined with translucent glass tops. *Metropolis* model by Interi.

Square wooden center table with metal rivets, 1930s-style. From Roche & Bobois.

Center table with metal legs and glass top. A classic designed by Alvar Aalto.

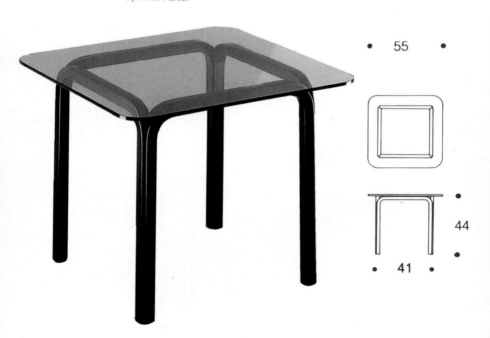

• 55 •

44

• 41 •

Small beech side cabinet with exposed hinges. Design by Habitat.

Opposite: Low table with casters and top made of *anigré* veneered composite board, dyed a mahogany color and varnished. The casters are made of steel and rubber. This is the *Scuadra* model from Habitat.

Below and right: Black lacquered table with Japanese-style decoration. Design by Habitat.

Original wooden center table. Design by
Raíz Cuadrada of Interi.

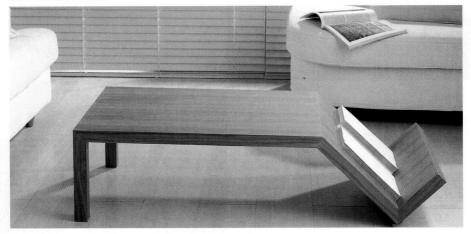

Couches with three or more seats

Two couches facing each other with a center table between them form an area especially suited to long conversations.

In brightly lit spaces large couches represent an option which allows for more than one conversation area.

Classic structure for a meeting area. The suite of couch and armchair dominates the entire space.

Corner couch in chaise longue style combining cushions in various colors. *Jules et Jim* model by Moroso.

Couch unit made up of a number of
elements: straight couches, corner
modules, divans, round modules,
curved couches, armchair and pouf.
Design by Roche & Bobois.

Couches with three or more seats 95

Couch unit with two large round modules, an arm, and a round cornerpiece. Design by Roche & Bobois.

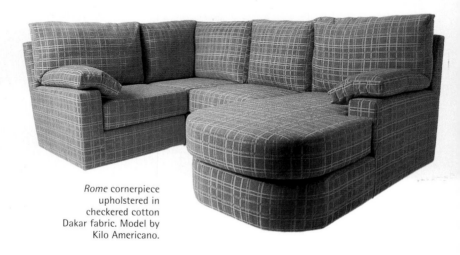

Rome cornerpiece upholstered in checkered cotton Dakar fabric. Model by Kilo Americano.

Couch unit composed of several elements:
straight couches, corner modules, divans,
round modules, curved couches, armchair, and
pouf. Design by Roche & Bobois.

A solid structure and very soft seating are the distinguishing characteristics of *Basiko*, a large couch with plain upholstery. Basiko from B & B Italia.

Framed *London* design by Matthew Hilton, with turned wooden legs, and seats and back in polyurethane. Model by Perobell.

With the *Balillo* series of couches, Antonio Citterio has achieved a concise synthesis of tradition and modernity. The contrast between the cushions and the structure is dazzling. Model from B & B Italia.

Three-seater couches in wood and metal covered with polyurethane and protective fabric. Metal legs. *Metropolitan* design by Alberto Lievore for Perobell.

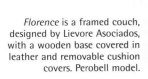

Florence is a framed couch, designed by Lievore Asociados, with a wooden base covered in leather and removable cushion covers. Perobell model.

Opposite: Apartment almost entirely decorated with stainless steel. The couches, next to the staircase, follow smooth straight lines.

Appearances

The living room as a whole must maintain a harmony, and this will be defined by the architectural elements, the furniture available, and the point chosen as the central nucleus. The room must respect the color scheme and follow the logic of its textures. Small details can be supplied by the lighting and other items of decoration.

Conversation area with metal-legged couches. The elegant frames of the windows match the rest of the decoration.

Living room in the residence of the architects Zorn de Krueck and Sexton. Avant-garde furniture with very modern lines was chosen to unify the setting.

The soft, warm ocher tones represent a distinctive element in this living room, separated from other areas by a DM partition. *Casa Margarida*: Aranda, Pigem, Vilalta Architects.

Wicker, wood and natural fibers unify this living room dominated by large windows, with transparent drapes which filter the light. *Charlotte House*, designed by Günter Behnish.

The *Lawson-Westen House* by Eric Owen Moss is defined by its structural elements. These form the basis for the decoration of the living room, taking into account the black and honey tones of the wood.

Optimizing space

Modern spaces tend to camouflage furniture by incorporating glass in center tables and bookcases. Setting by Matteo Grassi.

We are living through a period of synthesis between the demands of the market and the needs of use, with important consequences in the world of decoration. Furniture is not as high as it was traditionally, because it is being designed with the idea of avoiding obstacles which impede an overview of a space. Even pieces of furniture which go against the wall, such as bookcases and sideboards, are smaller. Furthermore, there is a trend toward using materials which do not reduce the sense of space. This is particularly true of glass, which is often used for secondary table tops and storage units.

The use of white and aluminum allows for very open compositions in furniture intended for storage. *Sapporo* collection from Stua.

Today's chairs are designed with a tubular structure and low backrests. *Frog* design by Piero Lissoni for Living.

Pale-colored wooden bookshelves fit perfectly in modern settings and are not visually oppressive. *Space* by Matteo Grassi.

Oriente is an armchair with steel bands and a high back with rounded shapes. Design by B & B Italia.

This surface furniture is distinguished by the sharpness of its lines. The only element which modifies its volume is the legs, in wood or nickel-plated steel. *Apto Collection* by Maxalto.

Modular systems make it possible to separate units to get the most out of a space. *Box* model by Living.

A wide modular bookcase set against the wall saves space, and this effect is enhanced by its finishing in dark colors and the use of beveled glass. From B & B Italia.

Side tables, stools, and benches with thin, nickel-plated steel legs benefit from a very airy and light design. From Maxalto.

Bookcase in a very versatile cocoa color which occupies very little space. From Maxalto.

A modular bookcase can have a space set aside for housing audio-visual equipment. Composition in wood and glass with metal lacquered pearl gray. Design by Galli.

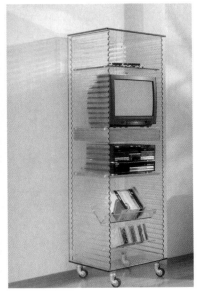

Sound and image

Audio-visual equipment has become the new protagonist of living room decoration. Designers have created useful pieces of furniture, containers and trolleys, either to emphasize it or to camouflage it.

Trolley for CD/videocassettes in varnished soldered metal tubing. It can be used in several positions and is designed for both CDs and videos. It can also take hi-fi equipment and a television. *Onda Radio Due* is a Ron Arad design for Fiam Italia.

Onda Kart container in rippled glass with adjustable shelves. It has casters to facilitate its movement. A Ron Arad design for Fiam Italia.

A modular bookcase containing a space specifically designed for the television. Design with a walnut finish by Interi.

Left: Wall cupboard for CDs, made of lacquered metal and beech. *Sund* model from Ikea.

Robin is the creation of Knut Hagberg and Marianne Hagberg for Ikea. It has thick shelf edges in birch color.

Compac by Interi is a multi-functional piece of furniture which can accommodate both a bookcase and an element specifically designed for the television. *Pescante* model by Interi, with metal legs and a walnut finish.

Square side table
with a solid fir base
and a beech veneer.
Peso for Habitat.

Audio-video unit with a
composite board structure
and a cherry veneer. Sliding
doors made of tempered
glass. Design by Habitat.

Modern low pieces of furniture
with steel legs are suitable for
supporting television sets, and
fit perfectly into the overall
decoration of the living room.

Horizon 547 makes it possible to keep the television and the video in a restricted space. Design by Willem Sterken for Leolux.

Kaleidos 540 container for sound and image, designed by Axel Enthoven for Leolux.

The *Penta* side table
in solid beech with
aminoplastic varnishing,
on a hand-woven *Galette*
model rug. Habitat.

Ciack TV, designed by Elli &
Moltoni for Porada, is a
television trolley in walnut, with
a black metal structure. The
lower level has arches in
textured black metal.

An old brick wall decorated with an abstract painting serves as the starting point for the creation of a modern living room, with voluminous couches and a glass center table. Design by Moroso.

Centers of attention

Meeting or conversation areas must, as far as possible, be situated close to one of the living room's natural centers of attention, such as the biggest window or the fireplace. If this is not possible, then the area must make its own signature, with a different type of flooring, for example. The other parts of the living room will take on a secondary role, with different furniture, but it is essential that the overall decoration should have an esthetic coherence.

A wide window with wooden frames allows sunlight to enter this large space, presided over by a three-seater couch and an armchair. Moroso.

An antique painting has served as a reference point for the positioning of the couch, which is upholstered in beige to complement the elegant setting. Design by Moroso.

Walls with arches and ribbing are the focus of attention for an original and modern living room. Design by Matteo Grassi.

A rug, which serves as a reference point, dominates this setting, lit by a large window. Designs by Matteo Grassi.

The fireplace is often the center of attention in a living room, and can give rise to a cozy setting. Design by Moroso.

A beveled glass panel with a beech wood frame serves as the starting point for the decoration of this small area, containing a couch with metal legs and lemon yellow upholstery. Design by Moroso.

Some pictures leaning against the wall are the center of attention in this setting. The couch with its sensual shapes fits in front of them. Design by B & B Italia.

The use of glossy metallic
materials in the bookcases
accentuates the linearity of
this roomy living room.

he predominance of the straight line

Current forms are tending to be more refined but,
with a few exceptions, the overall look is
dominated by straight lines and their variants,
even in the work of designers that seems softer
because the hardest edges are beveled and curved.
False straight lines in a piece of furniture also
provide more congenial settings and permit
combinations which achieve intimate atmospheres.
However, this refinement of lines leads to stylized
volumes, which of necessity are also close to the
straight line.

Armchair with wood frame and
straight lines leading to chromed
aluminum legs. *Box*, designed by
Piero Lissoni for Living.

Living room with stylized forms,
including a large, low wooden
table. Setting by Living.

Shelf unit made of elliptical laminated steel tubes. Supports and bookrests in natural beech finish. It is designed by Gabriel Teixidó for Enea.

Easy chair upholstered in leather with tubular aluminum legs.

Gray and cream tones make very simple lines of compact furniture and objects stand out. By Leolux.

The *Waldorf* two-seater couch, designed by Roberto Lazzeroni, is made of wood covered with rigid polyurethane.

Glass shelves with metal supports create a linear effect that enhances the space. Design by Matteo Grassi.

Display cabinet with frosted glass doors. Model by Stua.

Couch with a high arm and a squared line, which stands out on account of its covering. The cushions are complemented by typical bolsters. *Baisity* model from B & B Italia.

Furniture of distinction: the chaise longue and the footstool

Antique divans and footrests are being updated with original shapes and daring fabrics.

Pouff Papua which converts into a bed. From Kilo Americano.

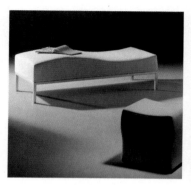

Agua Relax is a minimalist pouf with a removable cover. It has a metal base powder-coated with aluminum and varnished. It is designed by Diego Fortunato for Perobell.

Opposite: Large footrest with aluminum legs, upholstered in blue crushed velvet. *Charles* model from B & B Italia.

Chaise longue upholstered with floral motifs, on casters for greater mobility. From Roche & Bobois.

Chaise longue
with an
armrest.
Casablanca
model from
Kilo Americano.

Pouf
upholstered in
white, with
cocoa-colored
wooden legs.
From *Dialogica
en Aspectos.*

Chaise longue with wooden legs, and
a comfortable cushion for resting the
head. *Metropolitan* design by
Perobell.

A large chaise longue with a
practical armrest has been
positioned next to a bookcase.

Chaise longue designed in cord or transparent PVC with cotton cushions. The tubular frame is made of epoxy powder coated metal. *Frog* from Living Divani.

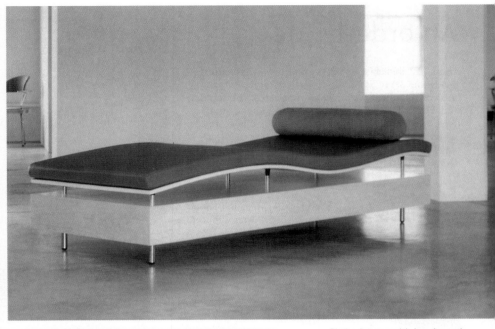

Chaise longue with beechwood legs. *Club Collection New Classic* from Cyce.

Chaise longue with a wooden base and metal legs, designed by Maya Lin for KnollStudio.

An orderly life

The latest bookcases offer a great deal of storage space and serve as multipurpose containers which are very practical in the living room area. The trend today is to make them open, or with modules that have functional sliding or folding doors made of wood or glass. They do not take up much space, are not heavy, and use aluminum or steel as a support. Note their useful casters.

Bookcase with vertical separations made of composite board veneered with varnished beech. *Adelfi* model from Habitat.

Bookcase unit
in pale wood,
set off by the
darker shade
underneath the
multifunctional
shelving.
Design by
Matteo Grassi.

Opposite: *Argento vivo* bookcase unit with a cocoa-colored finish. *Zona Giorno* collection for Galli.

Bookcase with a wenge finish, including a glass case for storing crockery. *Aura* design by Interi.

Bookcase that combines ebony and beech tones. *Isola* design by Bisana.

Moda bookcase in stained and varnished beech with eight shelves made of tempered glass. A model from Roche & Bobois.

Modular bookcases in injected aluminum with a metallic silver finish. The glass shelves are extremely sturdy and the wall brackets are made of smelted aluminum finished in metallic silver. *Naos* design by Gabriel Teixidó for Enea.

Shelf in frosted glass with decorative supports in chromed metal. Design by T. Colzani for Porada.

Above: A glass bookcase with aluminum supports creates a useful storage space behind a leather couch. Design by Roche & Bobois.

Left: Modular bookcase in cherry wood, with casters fitted with individual brakes.

Small side table in
beechwood with a
natural varnish, and a
practical drawer
incorporated. Habitat.

Smart furniture

There are some useful pieces of furniture
that help to round off the decoration with
a little extra originality and elegance.

Atena is a CD rack in
cherrywood and chromed
metal, with a curved
wooden support. Porada.

Small piece of
furniture designed
to store objects
and display items.
It is made of
natural beech
with steel handles.

Pochino stool in wood with
aluminum legs. Design by
Hans Peter Weidmann
for Artek.

Bar furnishing which can be used
as a low table or placed at the
end of the couch. Very mobile, it
is made of medium density
wood-fiber. Model from Habitat.

End-of-couch piece made of medium density wood-fiber. *Patty* model from an old Habitat collection.

Screen for separating areas.

Console table in a 1930s style, made of solid cherrywood with a honey hue, stainless steel, chrome, and a glass shelf. *Trocadero* by D. Ezan for Roche & Bobois.

Set of tables in solid cherrywood with an ornamental motif in curved wood. *Duetto* model by T. Colzani, from Porada.

Mini-bookcase in wood with a cherry veneer, with a sliding door and a retractable shelf. *Virgule* is designed by A. Gamba and L. Guerra for Roche & Bobois.

Luna is a useful little trolley in solid cherrywood with transparent glass levels fixed to the wooden structure. The handles are in chromed metal. From Porada.

Container hanging in the air. *Dama* unit in cherrywood with a frosted glass front. Finished in a cocoa color. Design by Galli.

Footrests can also
be transformed
into useful
center tables.

Original center tables

Often we do not need to resort to the traditional square or rectangular center table. There are many alternatives, such as trunks, footrests, boxes, rustic chests, and so on that can be perfect replacements.

A couple of boxes can be used as a table for putting down magazines or cups.

A trunk is functional as well as decorative for placing in the center or at the side of a set of easy chairs.

A small wooden sculpture serves as a support for works of art from Africa. Setting by B & B Italia.

An old wooden door serves as an original center table. Revolving casters have been incorporated to make it easier to move around.

Modular bookcase with aluminum legs. *Raíz Cuadrada* from Interi.

Multipurpose bookcases and modular units

The living room can also be used to keep or exhibit all kinds of objects, from domestic appliances to books and ornaments. The new modular units are versatile and can be adapted to suit all needs and all requirements. Their structures are light but very solid, and they use contrasting materials, such as frosted glass and tempered aluminum.

Panel doors, vertical sliding glass doors, a cozy space for the television and easy-to-open drawers define the new trends in modern bookcases. *Wall to Wall* model from Poliform.

Two photos, an overall view and a close-up. Mountable bookcase with a support for the hi-fi and television. Design by Grattarola.

Bookcase with rounded doors and synchronized opening, in wood with a birch veneer. It has five striking shelves. Design by A. Gamba and L. Guerra for Roche & Bobois.

Bookcase or display cabinet, with rustic-style paned glass. Design by Roche & Bobois.

Assembled *Bibliophile* unit with an imaginative range of elements, including wooden doors with glass panes, runners, curves, folding blocks, CD/video drawers, a bar, and halogen lighting. It is a creation of G. Gorgoni for Roche & Bobois.

Sapporo bookcase, designed by Jesús Gasca for Stua. It is a modular unit in white aluminum and shiny glass.

Metropolis is a modular ensemble designed by Antonio Citterio with a very flexible composition, sliding aluminum doors, and a birch structure. From Tissetanta.

Modular unit in a combination of woods with a frosted glass front and aluminum legs and handles. *Altamar* design from Interi.

Small *Quadratus* bookcase with a base in the form of a bench, which contrasts with the large size of the sliding doors. The shelves can be fitted out with aluminum accessories for videocassettes and CDs. Finished in Canaletto walnut and mat white lacquer. From Tissetanta.

Center tables

Novocomun. G. Terragni.

Café. Giacomo Passai.

Navigli. Calligaris.

Seven. Giacomo Passai.

Verona. Nancy Robbins.

Vulcano. Vico Magistretti.

Apta collection. Antonio Citterio.

Domino. Charles Rennie Mackintosh.

Par. L. Alba y J.M. Casaponsa.

Arabesco. Zanotta Spa.

Mesa centro. T. Mizutani.

Mesa *Phidea.* Pete Sans.

T-Jules. Moroso.

T-Big Mama. Moroso.

Olimpia. Sancal.

Prima. Sancal

Easy chairs

Three chairs of the *Tokyo* model. Nancy Robbins.

Bloody Mary armchair. Jordi Busquets.

Latin armchair.
Lover armchair.
Lucky armchair.
Gabriel Teixidó.

Bravo armchair.
Sergi & Oscar
Devesa.

Madison armchair.
Patricia Guiotto.

Basilea chair.
Ka International.

Galatea armchair.
Bros Contract.

Itaca seat.
Bros Contract.

Do Re Mi
armchair. Moroso.

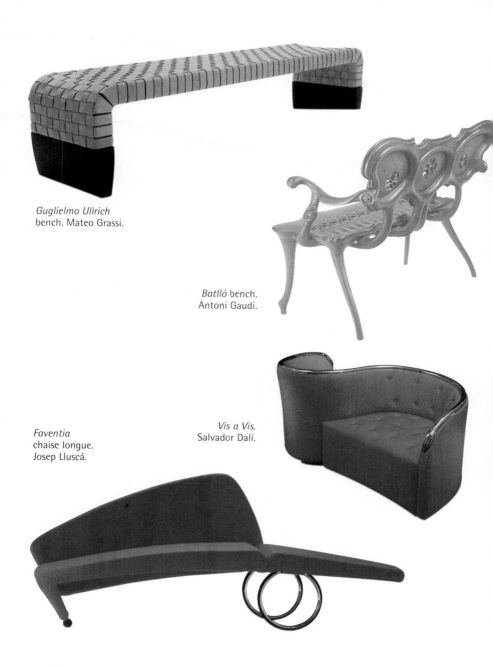

Guglielmo Ullrich
bench. Mateo Grassi.

Batlló bench.
Antoni Gaudí.

Faventia
chaise longue.
Josep Lluscá.

Vis a Vis.
Salvador Dalí.

Chair.
M. Brever.

Bogart armchair.
Giacomo Passai.

Metro armchair.
Estudi Metro.

Apta collection.
Antonio Citterio.

Ghost armchair.
Fiam Italia.

Couches and armchairs

Pelikan Desing. Fredericia Stolefabrik.

Monza armchair. G. Terragni.

Cubic. L. Alba & J.M. Casaponsa.

América. Moroso.

Guglielmo Ullrich armchair. Mateo Grassi.

Havana. Swan.

Portland. Swan.

Wind. Swan.

Borghese. Swan.

Tamigi. Moroso.

Jelly. Piero Lissoni.

Strömstad. Ikea.

Easy. Moroso.

Waldorf. Roberto Lazzeroni. Moroso.

Burnham. Laura Ashley.

Osborne. Laura Ashley.

Margot. Swan.

Mimmy. Massimo Losa. Moroso.

Mortimer armchair. Laura Ashley.

Burnham armchair. Laura Ashley.

Denbigh Leather armchair. Laura Ashley.

Club armchair. Moroso.

Rotor. Enea.

Cabriolet. Enea.

Club. Moroso.

Bejar armchair. KA International.

Barcelona armchair. KA International.

Bari armchair. KA International.

Bilbao armchair. KA International.

Denbigh armchair. Laura Ashley.

Brecon armchair. Laura Ashley.

Kreta armchair. Sancal.

Avaniko Plus armchair. Sancal.

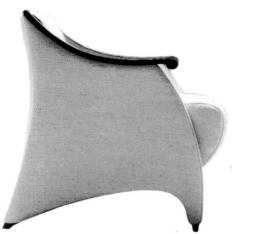

Taif armchair. Sancal.

Florence armchair. B & B Italia.

Valmont armchair. Sancal.

Gluan armchair. Marc Newson. Moroso.

Chicago armchair. Cycsa.

Dining rooms

The classical model for a dining room demanded — and still demands — uniformity in the furnishing. It was as if everything made up a single piece in which the table, the chairs, and the other furniture were inseparable. Moreover, whether or not they were being used, they had to be prepared for their exclusive function at all time. The present-day dining room — or at least the modern one — normally combines several styles; it is highly versatile and can be set up and put away again. This flexibility means it can serve everybody's needs in any situation or at any time.

As there is not normally any surplus space in modern houses, more and more homes are dispensing with an independent dining room and adapting that room for several uses (living/dining room, kitchen/dining room, dining room/workroom). These kinds of rooms are not difficult to furnish: the dining area only requires a table and some chairs that go well with the rest of the space. In any case, whatever the space available for eating, there are some questions that have to be answered before going on to furnish it.

Of course, we must first decide whether it will be a place exclusively for eating or whether it will also serve other purposes; also, how many people will regularly use the dining room; the maximum number of diners who will eat there, and whether space must be given over to the storage of any kind of accessories (crockery, table linen, etc).

The layout of a dining room — as for most other rooms in the home — must take as its starting point the dimensions and shape of the floor. This is the safest way of ensuring that the decisions taken are the correct ones. The dimensions of the floor indicate how much space is available, which means that we can settle straight away what furniture is appropriate for the room. The shape of the floor gives us a rough idea of how we can arrange the space, and it also shows what kind of table is best for the space. The table must always be a reflection of the dining room floor, and that will help us to

decide if it has to be square or rectangular — although, of course, there is always the option of a round table, which is much more versatile. In a dining room everything revolves around the table. If the room is used exclusively for eating, the table can be placed in the center, but it should not obstruct people's comings and goings. Normally, however, it is better to put it on one side, or in one corner, or against a wall.

When choosing a table, be aware that there are some measurements that have to be taken into account. When you are buying both table and chairs, first sit at the table. Check that the height is appropriate, and, if the chairs have arms, make sure that they fit the table. Each seat is around 26 inches (65 cm) wide, plus 2 inches (5 cm) if the chair has arms. The width of the table should therefore be at least 30 inches (75 cm). A rectangular table for six diners must be at least 52 inches (130 cm) long; for eight, it must be 82 inches (210 cm). The diameter of a round table can range from 40 inches (1 m) for four seats, to 60 inches (150 cm) for a large family.

The chairs can be set round the table, but it is better to have them dispersed. If we have enough room and have good furniture, we must buy chairs which match the setting; it is worth having them big and comfortable. We must not forget that the use to which they are put means that they will easily get dirty, so, if they are upholstered we must make sure that the fabric is washable and durable. If not, we could find that the covering has to be replaced very frequently. Some models have separate cushions which can be dry cleaned when they get dirty.

If there is a sideboard or other furniture, this has a great bearing on the space. Normally it is put against a wall, but sometimes it can be used to separate different areas, creating an imaginary wall between the dining room and the living room. When this piece of furniture is high, it predominates visually over the table; in this situation, it must always be placed against the wall facing the natural light source (usually the window).

Chairs

The chair is designed for one
specific function, yet it is one
of the most used pieces of
furniture, and the only one
that can really be moved about
easily. It is an extremely simple
item, and nearly all twentieth-
century designers produced at
least one model.

The use of structures made out of flexible
steel tubing revolutionized chair design in
the 1920s. The majority of modern
architects experimented with this material,
and came up with some of the most
popular models of the twentieth century.
On this page, pieces by Eileen Gray (top),
Marcel Breuer (above), Marc Stam (right);
on the opposite page, chair by
Mies van der Rohe.

Another of the materials characteristic of chairs in the twentieth century was laminated wood. Chairs by Charles Eames, Alvar Aalto, and Jesús Gasca.

The well-known *Ant* by Arne
Jacobsen for Fritz Hansen.

Wood lacquered in black and the Art Nouveau tradition. Top, two models from the early twentieth century by C.R. Mackintosh and Josef Hoffman. Below, two contemporary models by Sigurd Strom and Kisho Kurokawa.

Synthetic fibers and rounded forms. From top to bottom: the *Bohème* chair by Björn Alge, *Bluebelle* by Ross Lovegrove, the famous *Tulip* by Eero Saarinen, and two models from the Fasem company, *Crop* and *Rosa*.

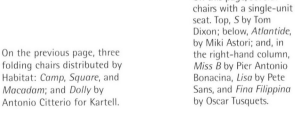

On the previous page, three folding chairs distributed by Habitat: *Camp*, *Square*, and *Macadam*; and *Dolly* by Antonio Citterio for Kartell.

On this page, several chairs with a single-unit seat. Top, *S* by Tom Dixon; below, *Atlantide*, by Miki Astori; and, in the right-hand column, *Miss B* by Pier Antonio Bonacina, *Lisa* by Pete Sans, and *Fina Filippina* by Oscar Tusquets.

Upholstered chairs. Top,
Greystoke by Alfredo Arribas
and *Nicola* from Habitat.
Below, *Marsina* by M.
Ramazzotti for Zanotta, *Fido* by
Toshiyuki Kita and *TV-Chair* by
Marc Newson, both for Moroso.

Temps by Jorge Pensi, for Punt Mobles.

Glass-top tables provide a visual extension of space and create beautiful contrasts with light forms.

Guests' dining room in the *Water and Glass House*, built in 1995 by K. Kuma in Shizuoka (Japan).

Glass tabletops

Like the home on the previous page, in this house – refurbished by the architects BDM – glass contrasts with the rough materials of the floor and the roof. Here, the dining room serves as an uninterrupted tunnel of light, between a courtyard and a garden, because of the effect created by the glass furniture.

Forgotten Lamp, designed by Pepe Cortés in 1976. The support is made of copper-plated iron and the lighting elements are made of chromed brass. From B. d.

This dining room, in a house designed by Tonet Sunyer in 1997, combines tradition and modernity. On the one hand, the roof with a typical Catalan dome, and the chairs and mat made of vegetable fibers; on the other, the glass table with steel legs on casters, and the lamp by Pepe Cortés.

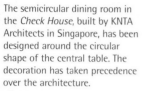

The semicircular dining room in the *Check House*, built by KNTA Architects in Singapore, has been designed around the circular shape of the central table. The decoration has taken precedence over the architecture.

The dining room in this house built by Rob Wellington Quigley in 1994 is dominated by a Klein painting.

When the famous French architectural couple Gilles Jourda and Françoise Perraudin built their own house near Lyon, they furnished it with pieces designed by modern masters, especially Le Corbusier. A glass table by Le Corbusier also appears in the dining room in the house built by Campi & Pessina in Montagnola.

Above and right: Two examples of glass tabletops which have been treated with acid.

Dining room in the
Villa Wachter in
Antwerp, by Jo Crepain.

Globus chair by Jesús Gasca for Stua.

The glass tabletop gives an impression of space.

In this house in the Tateshina Wood designed by Kazuyo Sejima, the feeling of space takes precedence over the functional requirements of the dining room.

In the house designed by the Italian team Citterio & Dwan in Kumamoto, the large dimensions of the space (unusual in Japan) contrast with the use of traditional furniture. In the *Kidosaki House*, the Japanese designer Tadao Ando has done just the opposite: he inserts Western furniture into an architectural structure conceived as a geometrical abstraction of Japanese space.

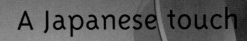

A Japanese touch

Minimalism and the almost total
absence of decorative elements
are the distinguishing marks of
the Japanese style.

Opposite: In this house, two completely different houses built by Yoshihiko Iida. The first, totally covered in wood, is that of a mountain house, whilst the second, looking out on to a courtyard, is in Tokyo. Here several pieces of European furniture can be seen, such as the *Arco* lamp by Achille Castiglioni and the *Ant* chair by Arne Jacobsen.

In these two houses by Naoyuki Shirakawa, the dining-room table looks out on to an inner courtyard through an enormous window.

Spacious dining rooms

Spacious dining rooms require special care in the choice of table and chairs, as they take on the characteristics of an isolated unit.

House in Bern, by Daniel Spreng.

House in Rome, by Massimiliano Fuksas.

The three dining rooms on this page benefit from extra high space just above the table. To contrast with the spaciousness of the setting, the furniture selected is particularly light and minimal. House in Le Véniset by Donati & Dubor.

Swiss houses beside a lake: *Walser House* by Luigi Snozzi and *Russ House* by Ernst Giselbrecht.

Casa Amat by Antoni de Moragas.

House on
Great Cranberry
Island by
Peter Forbes.
The generous
use of wood
aims to fit
out a warm
and cozy
space for the
harsh climate
of the area.

In the *Stremmel Residence*, built in 1994 by Mark Mack in Reno (Nevada), the size of the space affects the scale of all the elements. In particular, the dining room table is not a single table but two identical tables placed side by side.

The dining room in Steven Spielberg's house in the Hamptons, designed by Gwathney & Siegel, turns back to the traditional materials for country houses.

The house designed by Jaume Riba in Sant Jaume de ses Oliveres recalls the spatial layout and materials of the Barcelona Pavilion by Mies van der Rohe. However, the furniture is from the 1960s.

Putting the table next to a large window means that the dining room space seems to extend out into the landscape.

Dining room in the *Wabbel House* by Wolfgang Döring.

Famous chair designed by Mart Stamm. The work of Stamm, Breuer, and Mies with steel tube structures represented a revolution in chair design, insofar as they came to replace traditional legs.

The dining room in this Parisian apartment on Rue Dahomey, refurbished by Patrice Hardy, is lit by a large skylight. The white tiles on the floor, the white walls, the hanging piece of furniture, and the translucent chairs reflect light to the utmost. The vertical radiator stands out in this minimalist space, and almost seems to be a sculpture.

The dining room table in the Goldsborough loft in
London's Soho district, refurbished by A & M
Architects, is used not only for eating but also
for studying and working. A glass panel treated
with acid serves as a partition to separate the
dining room from one of the bedrooms.

Travertino marble table and chairs by
Hans Wagner in the dining room of the
Villa Neuendorf, built by John Pawson
and Claudio Silverstrin. The dining room
opens out on to a rectangular courtyard
enclosed by walls. In the Gaspar house by
Alberto Campo Baeza, the dining room
table lies between two identical
rectangular patios. Both houses represent
the most well known reference points for
the minimalist architecture of the 1990s.

Opposite: A table designed
by Antonio Citterio for the
Apta collection by B & B.

Functional simplicity

By staying clear of avant-garde designs, top manufacturers are creating dining room furniture of great simplicity and austerity with a strong visual impact, marked by an almost total absence of curves. Approaches to the design of the modern dining room tend to simplify lines as much as possible, with an ever increasing search for easy maintenance and comfort in use.

The *Aladino* collectio designed by Giacomo Pass for the Andreu Wor company, is based on simp and continuous lines us to make functional b attractive furnitur

The *Rima* chair, also designed by Giacomo Passal, with a more relaxed style and informal upholstery.

Classical structure for an ensembl of pure and stylized line Functionality and comfort in minimalist approac

Ensemble in simple lines from the Galli company. The dominance of the wooden tabletop is balanced by the plane of the seats, which emphatically avoid curved forms.

Simplicity and quality are t
outstanding attributes of t
design by Giacomo Pass

Opposite, bottom: Elegance a
functionality in the *Rima* moc
by Andreu World. The table
wooden structure is discre
and aims to coordinate t
entire space within a sinc
chromatic rang

Notorious series, designed by E.
Gottein and G.F. Coltella for Porada.
Made of wood, the ensemble is
somewhat stylized, with a single
ornamental detail in the finishing of
the armrests.

Calligaris offers an
updated design for one
of the most popular and
well-known chairs. An
avant-garde design for a
collection displaying
discreet elegance.

The architecture of
the *Aladino* chair is
dominated by two
arches which form
the fluid armrests.

Textures and motifs

The dining room and the combined living room and dining room are two areas which are very different, and their decoration has to be approached from opposing standpoints. An independent dining room can have a more showy design, with intense colors, a wealth of motifs, and an abundance of accessories. In a dining room incorporated into a living room, on the other hand, the color scheme is subordinate to that of the main room.

The combination of textures can mark out different areas of the house. The dining room area acquires a separate personality, thanks to a combination of classical textures and details set off by a rug. The contrast with the rest of the decoration implies that it is a space in its own right.

Dining room in the *Milledge Residence*. The presence of pale-colored Jacobsen chairs, contrasting with the dark shades of the table, creates a visual focus which lends character to the setting.

The building's structure is the principal motif for the design of this interior, and it gives character to the table area.

The spectacular architecture of *Russ House*, the work of Ernst Giselbrecht, takes pride of place in a setting designed to be functional.

Modern elements are placed in a rustic setting to express illogical surrealist ideas. The sobriety of the dining room elements contrasts with the other decoration.

"S" House, the work of Toyo Ito, consists of prefabricated pieces which shut off spaces and give them their individual, distinctive personality. The irregular shape of the dining room table reflects the original character of the whole house.

The individuality of this dining room with respect to the other parts of the home is enhanced by a self-contained color scheme, which imbues all the elements with its personality.

A totally integrated coordination gives the dining room area a subdued look, which enables it to blend into its environment.

Umberto Riva is the architect of *Casa Insignia*, where this dining room provides a total contrast in tones and styles. The antique-style chairs dominate a space characterized by its extreme simplicity.

Dual-purpose decoration

There are two main trends in the decoration of a dining room: the first consists of maintaining a strict functionality and only using a range of colors, textures, and finishings particularly suited to small rooms. The second approach highlights the difference between the living room and the dining room with contrasts that impinge on the independent character of each area.

Balú is a design by Giacomo Passai for the Andreu World company that uses a single chromatic range. The wall, with its bricks dyed white, boosts the personality of this space and separates it from the living room area.

Claudia ensemble by Giacomo Passai. Totally independent from the living room, this dining room asserts its individuality through the coordination of all its elements.

Jorge Pensi is responsible for *Sutil*, an ensemble made of wood and metal with a functionality reminiscent of designs for diners. The link-up with the kitchen separates this dining room from the living room, allowing the latter to assert its own personality.

This sideboard, elegant and discreet, mirrors the dark green tones of the chairs in its top level.

New versions of the sideboard

These days there is a greater coordination of the elements within a dining room, including, at least in materials and forms, the piece of furniture used for storage – if there is one. The current versions of the old sideboard are modular, and designers also use aerodynamic forms, top quality solid woods, and metal and glass with various kinds of finishing.

The *Navigli* sideboard from Calligaris.

Two large structures made of Italian walnut create a symmetry on both sides of this dining room by Tissetanta.

The *Apta* collection from Maxalto, the work of Antonio Citterio. The simplicity of forms and the sober finish characterize an element designed to reign over the living-dining room.

Galli is responsible for this sideboard, finished off with a translucent glass front. Its strong horizontal lines make it ideal for putting under a window.

Classical approach to a linear sideboard. Covered with white lacquer, and with a cherrywood top, its functionality complements its visual discretion.

The *Navigli* model from Calligaris. Made of natural ash with a glass top, this sideboard, by its very nature, demands a corner of the dining room to itself.

Although there is a trend toward smaller models, Galli presents this model in the *Dama* collection. The linearity of its structures confers elegance and serenity as well as functionality on a dining room.

Table for two. Simplicity of forms and schematic functionality in an ensemble of the *Milano* table designed by Josep Mora, and *Egea* chairs from Jesús Gasca.

The best choice

Not only must the furniture chosen for the dining room be visually attractive, but it must also correspond to the characteristics and dimensions of the room, ensuring that there is always enough space to get past the chairs and that the diners can be seated in comfort.

The square shape of the *Quadrotto* table, endowed with a great visual and formal simplicity, provides guests with great comfort and space.

Tavolo 95 is a design by Achille Castiglioni based on a highly functional and attractive structural simplicity.

The rustic atmosphere of this room is the overriding element in the simple and functional decoration of all its elements.

The round table structure accommodates a greater number of guests in a space free of any dead corners. Note the simple form of the sideboard in this combination, which does not overpower the setting.

In a perfect circle

Dining room tables can be round, oval, square, and rectangular. Round tables seat more guests than rectangular ones, and they also enhance conversation. Those with a central support leave more legroom, although they are not as stable as ones with four legs.

Andreu World presents this design by Giacomo Passai under the name *Calpe*. Functionality and comfort in an ensemble with simple lines.

Zanzibar marks a distance from traditional designs, in which tables only serve as supports for objects. Here the table takes on the additional practical function of a container.

Zero is a design clearly dominated by the curve. The backs of the chairs are coordinated with the tabletop, in both materials and form.

Close-up of the *Calpe* chair by Andreu World. The curve of the backrest coordinates the forms and gives the piece a character of its own.

In *Check House*, an architectural commission by the KNTA group, the table, made of glass, seats ten. Its avant-garde design reflects its modern, rational setting.

Vico Magistratti is responsible for this ensemble, featuring the *Shine* dining room table. Visual elegance in a simple and well balanced design.

This tabletop for the *More* model, supported by stylized cylindrical legs, has two sidepieces made of frosted glass flanking a central transparent section.

Dining room tables

Sistema SP table.
Alberto Lievore y
Asociados.

Mayra table. Chueca.

Versus table.
Giacomo Passai.

Wooden table. BD.

Pitavola table.
Lievore Asociados.

Victoria table.
Mateo Grassi.

Diedro table.
Roberto Barbieri.

Enterprise table.
Calligaris.

Table. Jorge Pensi.

Risico Basic table.
Calligaris.

Albert table.
Calligaris.

Aventino table.
Calligaris.

Elemental table.
L. Alba & J.M.
Casaponsa.

Obelisco table.
L. Alba & J.M.
Casaponsa.

T-Square table.
Moroso.

T-Waiting table.
Moroso.

Table. Klaus Bergen.

T-Sem table. Moroso.

Globus. Jesús Gasca.

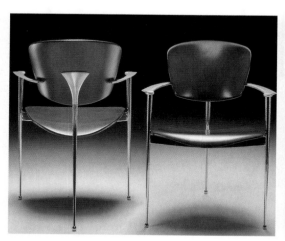

Andrea. Josep Lluscà.

Kion. Indecom/Just Meyer.

Jorge Pensi.

Lia. Roberto Barbieri.

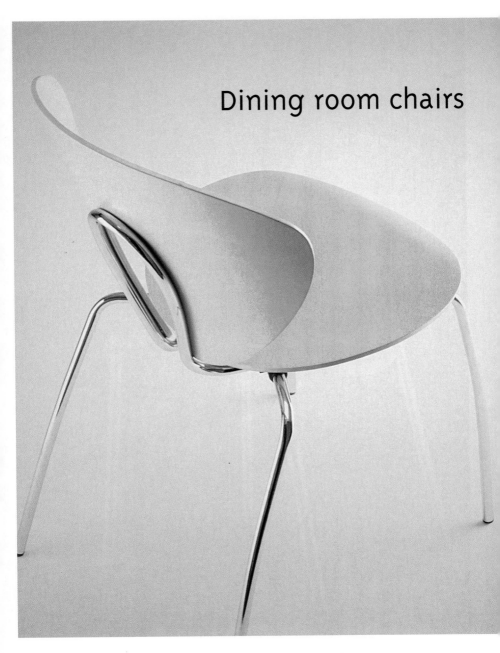

Dining room chairs

Global. Josep Lluscá.

Knoll.

Trazo. Sancal.

Melandra. Antonio Citterio.

Pluto. pouf. Promemoria.

Tíscar. Carles Tíscar.

Onda. Juan Montesa.

Madeira. Giacomo Passai.

Divino. Pete Sans.

Bittersüss. Mateo Grassi.

Claudia. Giacomo Passai.

Fullerina. Mateo Grassi.

Fullerina FLO 3. Mateo Grassi.

Milenium. Calligaris.

Guglielmo Ullrich. Mateo Grassi.

Principe. Calligaris.

Canova. Calligaris.

N.Y. Calligaris.

Pará. Calligaris

Vanity. Calligaris.

Movie. Calligaris.

Sideboards

Apta collection. Antonio Citterio. Maxalto.

Guglielmo Ulrich. Mateo Grassi.

Sistema. Grupte.

Contenedor Elemental. Estudi Metro.

Neguri. L. Alba & J.M. Casaponsa.

Apta collection. Antonio Citterio. Maxalto.

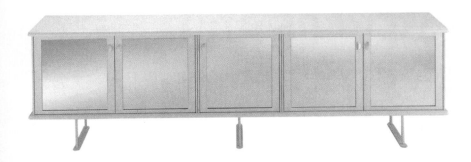

Bonn. Enzo Mari.

Util. L. Alba y J.M. Casaponsa.

Kitchens and electrical appliances

The kitchen is one of the most frequently visited parts of the house. It is where food is prepared and dishes are washed; sometimes it is used for eating, and people are going in and out all the time. This means that, when decorating, functional considerations must be taken into account just as much as decorative ones.

The ideal kitchen is one that best suits our needs, that makes the best use of the space available, and respects the architecture of the home. There is a wide variety of styles to choose from: the avant-garde kitchen, combining the warmth of wood with state-of-the-art techniques; the colorful kitchen; the technological kitchen, semi-industrial in style, with steel as the primary material, or the natural kitchen, suitable for both town and country, that uses material like cherrywood, beech, and teak.

The layout of any kitchen largely depends on the space available; the elements can cover two facing walls, form a U shape, or be in one row. If space permits, it is also possible to have a central working area. Whatever we decide upon, the following considerations must not be ignored: it is important that the most used elements — the cooker, sink, and electrical appliances — are fairly close to each other, and, if their standard height is inconvenient, we should raise them with a platform.

The sink is the most complicated component to change, due to the number of pipes, so it is cheaper not to transfer it somewhere else. As regards the work surfaces, they must jut out slightly to be easier to clean, and there must be one on either side of the cooker. The wear and tear inflicted on these surfaces means that we must opt for a high-quality material. These days there are some that combine natural and synthetic products, such as high-pressure laminates that are cheap and easy to clean. More costly are those made of woods like beech and teak, which are very attractive but require constant upkeep. Another expensive surface is marble; this has the advantage of being easy to clean and is very pleasing visually. Stainless steel is also very easy to clean, and it combines perfectly with other materials and is very resistant. One more traditional option would be tiles, but these could break when something heavy falls on them so always keep some spares.

Another surface that can cause worries about the right material to use is the floor. There are a number of materials to choose from: tiles, cork, rubber, or linoleum, amongst others. In the kitchen above all there is no ideal floor, and our decision must take into account the cleaning factor. A beautiful floor that is not hard wearing can give us many headaches once the initial shine has worn off.

However, what gives a kitchen life and joy is undoubtedly light. Most kitchens are not blessed with sunlight, so we shall need artificial light if we want to create a bright and pleasant space. To have more light in the kitchen, choose the right lamps and a combination of pale colors. Dark colors absorb light and make the room seem smaller. The work surfaces must be perfectly lit: the most common option is fluorescent tubes underneath the closets. It is also possible to create different atmospheres with halogen lamps set in the ceiling, which will enable us to personalize the table area and give it greater intimacy. Another option for this area is a lamp that moves up and down.

Electrical appliances have never before played such an important role in the kitchen. Ovens, vitroceramics, refrigerators, extractor hoods, washing machines, dishwashers, and microwaves join forces to improve our quality of life and make it easier to do the cooking, which is sometimes arduous after a hard day at work. All the companies making these products have put exceptionally designed avant-garde electrical appliances on the market. Apart from their appearance, we must make sure they are easy to clean, safe, quiet, fast, and enable us to save energy, detergent, and, most important of all, time.

Workspace

These days modern kitchens are designed with units made up of a wide range of functional elements. These modules are all removable and entirely visible.

The cooking center stands out in this module from Leicht. It has a granite top and a stainless steel extractor hood. The traditional wall unit has been eliminated to open up new dimensions in the layout.

An island with a stainless steel top.

Tables for informal meals

This section presents kitchen areas designed not only for preparing food but also for social gatherings. All these areas usually contain a table and chairs or stools set in the center to enjoy breakfasts, lunches, or quick informal dinners. An extendable table or a bar are other equally valid alternatives.

Two extremely different options. On the one hand, a wing-shape bar with two stools that have adjustable heights, from the manufacturer Sie Matic. On the other, a more traditional version, made up of a rectangular wooden table flanked by three cane chairs and a bench that will seat three people.

Once again, two contrasting options: one model by Sie Matic that evokes the atmosphere of a diner with a table/bar lacquered in black and high stools, and another by Alnopur that combines a table with a marble top and a designer chair by Phillippe Starck.

Tables set against the wall or partition to acquire space and greater freedom of movement, center tables with only two chairs in small spaces, tables designed as an extension of the main kitchen module, an American kitchen created by adding a bar that separates the narrow kitchen from the living room ... these are all viable options for including the dining room in the kitchen space.

Circular aluminum table with matching chairs, with a stainless steel structure and the seat and backrest in laminated metal.

A new possibility: a table on casters that means the space can adapt to any situation with ease. In these circumstances, it is advisable not to design any heavy structures that are difficult to move.

This new option combines the different proposals in this section. It consists of a main module with casters, which is also extendable, and a table top designed as an independent flap fixed to the wall. It is accompanied by metal-framed chairs with wooden seats and backs, from the *Zapping* series.

Secondary dining room table in a rustic style. The table has a fixed central wooden structure and two extendable side pieces in the same material. Drawers have been built in under the table to store table linen and the most frequently used cutlery.

Steel kitchens

Until recently steel kitchens were only found in restaurants, but in the last few years their use has been extended to the domestic setting. Some of the most well-known kitchen companies (Bulthaup, Boffi, Schiffini, etc.) make models with this material.

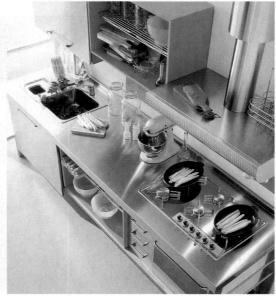

Assorted furniture

The work of the designer Peter Mally seeks to create furniture characterized by its absolute simplicity and clarity of line. This philosophy has led to Duo, an assemblage of containers, one of which is shown on this page: a square model with translucent glass doors, it is divided into compartments and fitted with drawers.

Sliding doors, plastic materials, original tile designs, combinations of colors, glass, wood, steel ... All these elements represent a summary of present-day trends in kitchen design.

Although wood is not generally used in kitchen design these days, it is the basic element in this model: floors, walls, tops, closets, drawers, doors, chairs – everything has been designed and built in the same type of wood.

Kuka model by Snaidero

The industrial trend is another of today's options. Designers are increasingly incorporating elements into the domestic setting that until recently were exclusive to big restaurant kitchens.

Designed by Blue Team, this *Byron* model is from the Schiffini series.

The furniture that breathes life into this setting come from the *Stua* collection. These original and practical elements make up a pleasant and warm ensemble. The bookcase is a *Sapporo* model; the *Zero* model table (designed by Jesús Gasca) has an aluminum top and a steel base. As for the chairs (also designed by Jesús Gasca), these represent the *Globus* model. They are light, elegant, stackable chairs, with attractive lines. The structure is stainless steel, and the seat and backrest are available in cherrywood, beech, ash, or maple.

Country kitchens

When trying to refurbish or install a country kitchen, it is important to weigh up the alternatives: although very simple lines are visually preferable, it is advisable to combine synthetic finishing in bright and cheerful colors with natural woods that have been stripped and stained in tones of oak, cherry, and beech.

SE 1001 KER model from Sie Matic. The ensemble is finished in oak that has been stained blue.

Alnoholm model from Alno. The furniture is finished in natural birch.

Opposite: Traditional tiles endow a country kitchen with good color and personality.

Rustic decoration
aims for intimacy
and warmth.

The modern rustic style is very fashionable these days. The wall, painted in warm tones, sets off the wood and gives the setting a touch of elegance.

To create rustic kitchen environments, a large working area must be created, topped with tiles and fitted with a smoke extractor.

Work surfaces are one of the most important features in a kitchen. These must be resistant because they are the most roughly used elements: they have to resist chopping, cold, heat, humidity, and grease, so the materials used have to be durable. The trouble is that wood is delicate, so zones of steel, granite, or marble must be created to reinforce the most heavily used areas.

The chest of drawers from a dry-goods store, the nineteenth-century metal containers, the glass bottles, the improvised composition of pots, lids, hooks, and chains: all these elements enhance the visual appeal so typical of country settings.

Militant modernity

Our lifestyle has changed enormously in the last few years, not only on a practical level but also in esthetic terms. These changes have obviously impinged on the design of today's kitchens. This section presents a representative example of "militant modernity."

This kitchen designed by
Storch & Ehlers (Hanover),
although unusual, is
exceptionally practical.

The flexibility of the *Metropolitan*
series lies in the possibilities it gives
customers of choosing made-to-
measure components.

Large kitchens

Reclaiming the kitchen as a large space
involves overcoming its image as a mere
service area. Living in the kitchen is only
possible if the space is bigger and better lit.

Two Poggenpohl kitchens in which the workspace occupies a central position.

a model
Leicht.

5003 unit by Eilin. Introducing furnishing better associated with other rooms, such as a bookcase, transforms the traditional image of the kitchen.

With views

The kitchen is traditionally a room where the walls are completely covered by the furnishings, creating the sensation of an enclosed space. This impression can be erased by focusing the work area toward a window, thus also enhancing the interior with the ever-changing mood and tone of light.

The kitchen is normally considered merely a functional space. Direct contact with the exterior adds the extra dimension of a pleasant atmosphere.

The presence of homely furniture and personal items gives this space a distinctive look, further enhanced by the light coming in from outside.

Colorists

Imagination is the key element in decoration with color. The application of color in design and decoration is extremely important: the suggestions on these pages offer just a few ideas and enticements for combining colors in the most important work area of the house.

Vola:
a cheerful interpretation of kitchen design.

Effeti Cucine:
Vola model. Colere.

Open plan kitchens

The absence of any physical boundaries creates large spaces in kitchens. Light, a prime consideration in the planning of a kitchen, is the protagonist in this ensemble in the Carmichael House, situated next to a staircase and facing the large window, which allows the pale colors to be set off by the variations in sunlight.

The area marked by the corner windows serves as the basis for this ensemble in the *Behnish House*.

This ensemble by
Enrique Norten is
designed to sit in the
middle of an open
space.

A kitchen opening out on the
dining room to take advantage
of the two large windows.
Cashman House.

Taking advantage of space

The adaptable shapes and sizes of today's kitchen elements mean that functional items with a great decorative appeal can be integrated into a restricted space. The use of an oval window, for example, and the coordination of the fronts of refrigerators and dishwashers demonstrate this adaptability.

Choosing the right elements, taking advantage of their functions, and making the most of corners are the key factors in kitchen design. Pale colors and simple lines enhance the luminosity of an interior kitchen deprived of light.

Natural wood

"Less is more." This is the overriding principle of the design in this section. The paler the colors and the more discreet the lines and forms, the nobler the material; imposing but warm wood combines with stainless steel to create a setting that is both welcoming and stately.

The *Ontario* model by Leicht is characterized by its modernity and naturalness. This elegant design, in wood with a maple veneer in silver and gold tones with solid wood borders, has the fronts of the drawers, veneered vertically.

The geometrical forms provide the perfect complement to the smoother lines. The cube-shaped elements in the paneled unit are all-purpose items from Sie Matic.

4003 unit in maple. From Sie Matic.

Bulthaup technology

The German company has always been in the forefront of design and technology in kitchen manufacturing. Nowadays, its kitchens tend to be conceived as laboratories for the preparation and treatment of foodstuffs.

Combinations of steel with wood, mobile modules, high-tech design, lacquered finishes, extractor hoods ... these are the ingredients of Bulthaup's success.

Magistretti kitchens

Italian design combines functionality and
esthetic rigor. The new kitchens are
characterized by versatility and elegance.

Clockwise: Schiffini series:
Cádimare model, *Solaro* model,
Cina model. Overleaf: Schiffini
series, *Campiglia* model.

The Boffi option ...

The Boffi (Bofficucine) program is characterized by its flexibility and discretion. It is centered around modular elements that reinvent kitchen furnishings and emphasize their functionality.

Mobile elements mean that the space can be distributed according to the demands of each occasion. Some of the designs incorporate sliding beechwood racks under the work surfaces, to hold trays, hanging baskets, and drawers.

... and the Citterio

The modern Italian kitchen: friendly, full of spontaneity, precision, and creativity. Designed and coordinated by Antonio Citterio, the Archinea collection reinterprets the elements of a great tradition. A unique way of designing and using space, time, and objects, and of testing the results of the prepared dishes.

Artusi kitchen unit, named after the most famous Italian cookbook writer.

Italia models: made-to-measure design based on space and practicality.

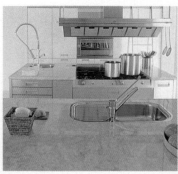

Kitchen closets

Sliding drawers, units hinged on a circular plane ... all these elements play a major role in creative and personal kitchen design. On the one hand, they have a great storage capacity; on the other, they have great visual appeal. The variety of forms, colors, and materials means that a kitchen can be uniformly decorated or offer sharp contrasts.

Above: Beech wood trolley with white plastic baskets (15 x 34 x12 inches; 38 x 87 x 30 cm).

Built-in closets are creative elements in the planning of a kitchen. Daring forms and contrasting colors give a personal touch to the design. Symmetrically placed semicircular closets (Sie Matic) and a curved in-built closet give a distinctive style to the kitchen. Tall thin closets provide a lot of space and are very accessible. Finally, strong, solid, quiet drawers, that are easy to handle are very convenient. Those of the Sie Matic company incorporate the Quadrotechnik system, which can resist weights of up to 25 pounds (12 kg) when totally extended and runs on tracks with ball bearings.

The new ovens

Automatic programming, internal temperature control, cold doors, self-cleaning and incorporated interactive screens: these are the defining characteristics of the whole new generation of ovens.

Low multi-function HEN oven. Q, Bosch.

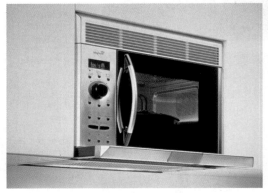

Microwave oven with *M.A.C.* extractor. Whirlpool.

Combiset unit, Miele.

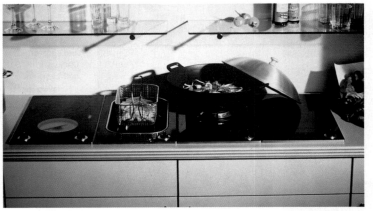

In-built oven, Miele.

Silver-gray *PR 8 IN* oven, Rosières.

Gas cooking plate *Gaggenau*.

Multi-function *FI 1029 IN* oven, Rosières.

Multi-function
independent
oven, *AKG
637/IX.*
Whirlpool.

Multi-function oven,
Oven Dialogic by Ariston.

Cocivap for steaming,
Imperial.

Convex oven with
tangential
ventilation, Candy.

Gaggenau
oven.

Microwave CIG 100,
built-in, Candy.

Built-in oven,
Gaggenau.

Washing machines and dishwashers

The latest models are connected to the Internet, have metallic finishes, and are camouflaged in kitchen units. Washing machines and dishwashers with front panels, built in under a work surface, are being incorporated more and more into modern kitchens to provide visual continuity in the furnishing design.

Washing machine WM 6147E, "Edition 150." Siemens.

2000 dishwasher. Ariston.

Margherita Dialogic washing machine, Ariston.

Built-in dishwasher, Miele.

Dishwasher,
7 programs, Candy.

Built-in
dishwasher,
Rosières.

Built-in dishwasher, Miele.

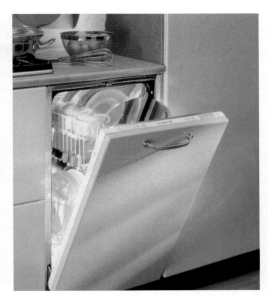

18-inch (45 cm) dishwasher, Rosières.

SE 25560 dishwasher,
Siemens.

Built-in
dishwasher,
Rosières.

Built Inn, Ariston.

Washer-drier, from Candy.

Dishwasher, Black
range, New Pool.

Dishwasher 2000,
Indesit.

The new extractors

The new extractors fit perfectly into the modern kitchen. The advantage of having a more recent model lies in its economy, comfort, and optimal absorption.

Retractable hood, Gaggenau.

AH 350–190 aspiration center, Fagor.

Steel extractor, Gaggenau.

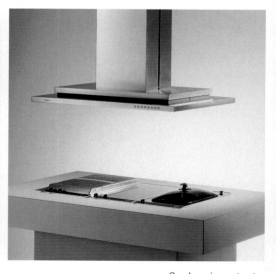

Overhanging extractor hood, Gaggenau.

Extractor hood with
glass shield, Miele.

Decorative extractor
hood, Miele.

Decorative
extractor hood,
Candy.

Overhanging
conical extractor
hood, Candy

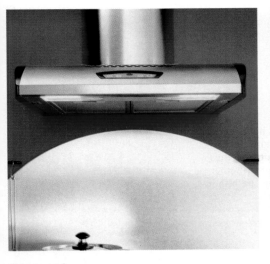

Chimney-style
extractor, Rosières.

Decorative extractor
hood, Rosières.

Decorative extractor hood, Fagor.

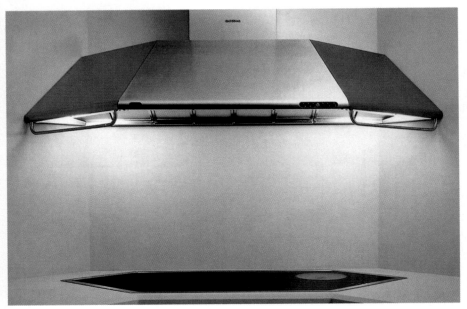

Refrigerators

One of the new trends in refrigerators harks back
to the 1950s look. There is a predominance of
metallic finishing, as well as astonishing novelties
like doors that change color according to whether
it is day or night. Controls for functions are also a
common feature.

Oz
refrigerator,
Zanussi.

Refrigerator and freezer built
in under work surface, Candy.

IK 300 refrigerator
and freezer center,
Gaggenau.

Wine rack
refrigerator,
Gaggenau.

Syde by Syde
Gaggenau.

Two-door
refrigerator with
incorporated
clock, Whirlpool.

Old Style refrigerator,
Rosières.

Two-door refrigerator, Candy.

Fr-700CB refrigerator, Daewo.

Old Style refrigerators, Rosières.

Vertical freezer, Ariston.

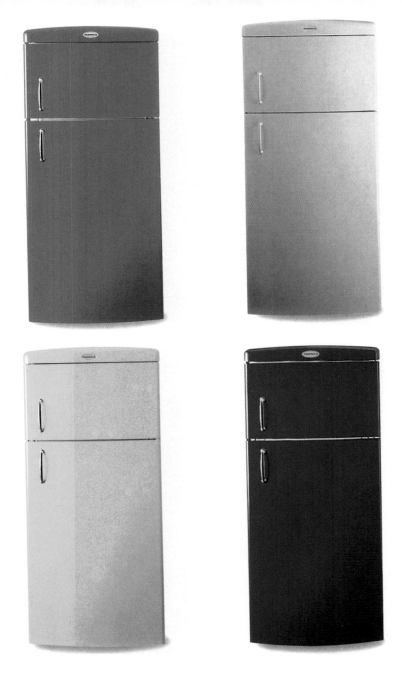

Refrigerator that changes color, according to whether it is day or night, Whirlpool.

Self Supporting refrigerator, Ariston.

Staircases

Staircases connect the various floors of a house. We use them a lot throughout the day, and so we should try to get them to fit our requirements and make them as suitable as possible for our needs. Above all, we must take into account the practical aspects. As for its design, whether we choose a curved staircase or a straight one, it is important that it blends in totally with the decoration of the space in which it is situated.

A staircase in a rustic living room will fit in perfectly with its setting if we use a material such as wood, whilst an avant-garde living demands a daring or innovative staircase. This is why architects and designers like devising staircases; it is an element that permits great creativity.

Nowadays, a variety of materials are used for constructing staircases: steel, translucent glass, solid wood, marble. When we are choosing what to buy, we must consider not only the price but also the quality and design. Each component of the staircase requires special attention. The size of the steps and the form of the handrails are subject to very strict legal regulations in some countries. If there are children or elderly people in the house, there is even greater reason to take care. There is a wide range of designs available for handrails, while the steps require a very resistant material as they are subjected to a lot of to-ing and fro-ing.

To ensure greater safety, and to avoid any falls or frightening trips, the steps must be well lit. The ideal solution is to put lamps on the staircase walls. Moreover, a staircase can acquire a personal character with the right lighting, and its visual impact can be greatly enhanced. On the other hand, if our staircase is blessed with sunlight, we can choose steps without any vertical panels, which helps to make the most of the natural lighting by allowing it to pass through the rungs.

We may choose to paint the wall adjacent to the staircase a more durable color than white, as we are dealing with a part of the house very liable to receive marks and knocks. It is more than likely that children will rub their

hands on the walls when they go up and down the staircase. However, it is important not to leave this wall completely bare. Pictures are the most common solution here. It is best to hang them vertically, since horizontal planes on a staircase are not particularly attractive.

We must not neglect the space underneath the staircase. If we leave this area undecorated, the setting will seem incomplete. We can take advantage of it to install a closet or lumber room, but if we do not need the area for storage space, we can fill it with a chest of drawers adorned with some of our favorite knickknacks. Another original and practical solution is the placement of a tatami and futon under the staircase, for use as a bed for that extra guest.

Plants and flowers are another valid option for brightening up the foot of the staircase; they can also decorate the steps themselves, and thus give life to the different levels.

If the house is narrow, the best form of staircase is the spiral. This type of structure allows sunlight to penetrate to all the floors, but, although it is true that a spiral staircase saves space, it is also less convenient than a conventional one.

These days staircases tend to be discreet, with simple lines; and even when they are sophisticated, they have lost the extravagance that characterized them in other eras. Putting a staircase into a house is no longer an arduous and expensive process requiring building work. In fact, it is now possible to install a staircase in around three hours, thanks to modular systems. These are generally prefabricated spiral staircases, in which each step is joined to the other by means of a central axis and the handrail is fixed to the steps.

Obviously, not everybody wants to turn their staircase into the center of attention in their living room, and some people do not like prefabricated designs with intricate and showy forms. Once again, the reference points must be the overall decoration of the room, the budget available, and the quality required in the product.

Straight to the living room

Many houses have staircases that descend straight into the living room, which acquires a great visual dynamism as a result by incorporating into its natural function the additional role of a distributor of space. By taking on these two functions, the living room is converted into a multiple space.

A simple style for a staircase that is built into a wall. The rustic decoration in the room below means that no decorative element is required on the staircase.

The various elements of this staircase mirror the colors in the living room.

The singular architecture in this house determines the organization of the living-dining room, with different levels joined by small tiered walkways, thus turning the staircase into the dominant feature of the space.

The curved form of this staircase descends into the dining area, and leads to the passageway formed by the couch.

In this living-dining room, two platforms differentiate between the eating and meeting areas. The staircase is coordinated with the steps linking these two zones, thus adding to the visual continuity.

A simple metal staircase opens out on two sides to increase the possibility of access. It is highly versatile, leading both to the living room and, on the far side, the hall.

From the hall

The hall is the most obvious place to put a staircase. In this case, the architecture takes pride of place, and decoration is a secondary consideration. Despite its simplicity, this area is spatially complex and versatile, as it leads on to all the rooms in the house.

Simplicity of line for a hall built entirely of wood. The placement of the staircase, in one corner of the space, increases the size of the passageways.

A piece of furniture with a number of shelves has been built into the bottom of this stairwell. This idea proves to be both attractive and versatile, as it takes advantage of the space while hiding the lower part of the staircase.

Access to the upper floor should be achieved without the need to cross rooms like the living room or dining room, and so the majority of staircases are situated in the hall.

The natural position for a hall is the center of the home. A hall with a staircase that has an overhead opening serving as a skylight.

Whether or not a hall has a staircase, it still requires the same kind of furniture and decoration.

In this area dominated by a large bookcase, the absence of doors is striking, as it opens up the space completely and offers great linear simplicity.

The stairwell

The stairwell is a space that usually measures no more than 10 square feet (about 1 sq. m), and therefore tends not to be decorated. However, the limited space should not allow the visual appearance of this area to be overlooked, as it is the only section of the staircase that can be decorated, thereby breaking up the monotony of the stairs.

This original office, in a classic style, has been situated on the upper part of the staircase.

The decoration of this intermediate area between two floors comprises a bookshelf with knickknacks and three pictures, which add dynamism and visual interest to the setting.

The most traditional solution for the stairwell is the wall lamp. It is of the utmost importance that lighting on the staircase enhances the atmosphere.

Studies, offices, and libraries

Our homes have specific rooms for different everyday tasks, but often a lack of space means that such fulfilling activities as reading and studying do not have a room to themselves. It is advisable for all schoolchildren and students to have their own space for studying, as this enhances their concentration, orderliness, and discipline.

However, it is not only students that need a study: people whose professions demand that they work at home also need one. If it is not possible to install a self-contained office in the house, than an appropriate space must be found in the living room, the bedroom, or any other available room. Some people even convert a suitably endowed space, such as a loft, into a study.

Books are indispensable in any study, but few people can permit themselves the luxury of giving over an entire room to them. The library must therefore be put in the study itself or, if this is not possible, in a corner elsewhere in the home. We do not have to put all the books together in one place, as we can divide them between the kitchen, living room, and bedroom. Books, regardless of what use we make of them, humanize a room and make it more welcoming. We must make sure that we keep our library in good order; one solution is to categorize books according to authors or subjects, and that way they are easier to find. Obviously, it is not a good idea to arrange them according to criteria of size and color.

However, libraries do not exist just to house books; they also contain audiovisual equipment and decorative objects, and can thus have a considerable visual impact. The ideal solution is a quiet and comfortable room with armchairs that entice us to sit down and read. Libraries can also be a good way of taking advantage of dead space in the home. They can

even be used to separate different areas, such as the hall and the lounge. Books can also cover the walls of a corridor, thus endowing it with a functional purpose. Whatever design we choose for our bookcases, it is important to opt for high quality, firstly because they must be strong enough to support a lot of weight; and, secondly, so that they will last longer.

A self-contained work area not only needs bookcases, but also other indispensable pieces of furniture, which must satisfy certain conditions.

Although surplus furniture can be recycled for use in the study, it is advisable for the office chair to be specially designed for this purpose. It must be comfortable, ergonomic, and save us from the back pains caused by bad postures. If it has casters it will afford us greater mobility. Armchairs are also essential in a study, because they offer us the relaxation we need to lose ourselves in a good book.

The office table should ideally be as big as possible, helping us to be efficient and to concentrate. It is important that it has drawers for storing work accessories. The ideal material for this piece of furniture is wood.

Moreover, the office can house other functional elements, depending on the interests and hobbies of the family. One example is the piano, which, apart from its obvious musical function, adds warmth to a room. Some people even decide to put a bar in their office. However, the element that is becoming increasingly commonplace is, of course, the computer, which has rapidly overtaken the typewriter.

Anybody who wants a cozy office dreams of having sunlight, as well as a fireplace to bring warmth to the space. Whether we have sun or not, it is always important to have suitable lighting. Some work tables already have a lamp incorporated, but if our choice does not we must install our own study lamp, in keeping with the design of the room. This sharply focused source of illumination must be complemented by more general ones, using spotlights or ceiling lamps to create diffuse but effective lighting.

A corner for the study

Any corner of the house can be fitted up as a study area. However, it is vital to make a careful evaluation of the characteristics of the space, especially the lighting and soundproofing.

In this house in Germany, Norman Foster has taken advantage of a landing on the staircase to install a work table in front of a large window.

In this London apartment, designed by Simon Conder, a bookcase and a work table separate the staircase from the lounge and serve as an improvised study area.

The type of material used (notebook or computer, watercolors or scanner) is decisive – not only in the final appearance of the study, but also in the placement of the table with consideration to the walls and the lighting.

The character and age of the users inevitably determine what type of study emerges. Also, the intensity of use will decide whether back-up elements like bookcases, trays, and chest of drawers are required.

Matching tables and chairs

A study area only requires an appropriate, well placed table and chair, although furniture usually associated with offices can clash with a domestic setting.

H2O unit designed by Bataille & Ibens for Bulo. The unit comprises a chair, desk, and filing cabinet.

The private study of the architect Enric Miralles. The table was specially made, while the chair is designed by Charles Eames for Vitra.

Table and chair from the Stua company. The *Milano* table is designed by Jesús Gasca, while the *Egoa* chair is by Josep Mora.

Two pieces by Vico Magistreti
for De Padova: the *Silver*
chair and the *Shin*e table.

A view of the *S House* designed by Toyo Ito for a couple of artists. The *Campus* chairs are designed by Fritz Hansen and made by Peter Hiort-Lorensen and Johannes Foersom.

Study in a house in Yokohama built
by Kazuo Shinohara, distinguished
by its striking furniture.

Office furniture by Pier Antonio
Bonacina and the *Miss* chair.

Opposite top: Extendable
Stilt table by Cozza &
Mascheroni and *Zip* chair by
Maran,
both for Desalto.

Opposite bottom: *Helsinki*
table by Caronni &
Bonanomi, also for Desalto.

Among books

These days it is a luxury to be able to use an entire room exclusively as a library. However, it is always possible to fill some corners with books, making them much more interesting and satisfying.

In these two studies, the main bookcase is situated right behind the work table.

In this Milan apartment refurbished by Franco Raggi, a made-to-measure bookcase separates the lounge from a small space packed with books. Raggi creates a great interplay between the various bookcases, using them as layers that go one behind the other.

This study is dominated
by the famous easy chair
of Charles Eames.

The bookcase in this extra high lounge does not reach the ceiling. The upper shelves remain empty, or are reserved for the books that are least consulted, such as the *S,M,L,XL* by Koolhaas.

A library without any excessive orderliness indicates more frequent use than one in which the books are neatly arranged. It is always advisable to classify books by subject or author, rather than arrange them by size or color.

Left and opposite: The end walls of these glass verandahs have been fitted out with bookcases, thus converting little used spaces into exceptionally well lit and very pleasant reading areas.

Working at home

The latest developments in the new technologies mean that more and more people can work at home, and domestic spaces are having to be transformed as a result.

Working at home requires an independent space suitable for business meetings, without disturbing the intimacy of the rest of the home.

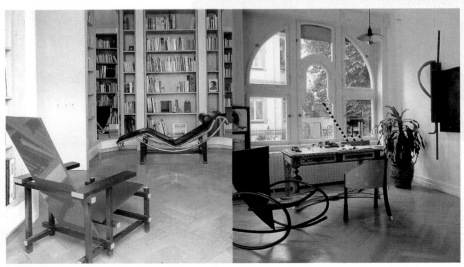

A spectacular study facing the North Sea in this
house built on the Jutland peninsula in Denmark
by Torsten Thorup and Claus Bonderup. Chairs
have been replaced by a stool designed by the
same architects, and marketed by Rapsel.

Rural study in San Diego, designed by Jeanne McCallum
and built almost entirely in wood: the structure, window
frames, furniture, ceiling, and so on.

The Jaume Tresserra office

Jaume Tresserra always works with top-quality materials, particularly walnut with natural varnishes applied by hand, with brass highlights. The simplicity of his sharply defined geometric forms is set off by extremely subtle details that contribute to the overall impression. Behind the apparent simplicity, an array of distinctive elements reveals a wealth of hidden possibilities: each gesture, each detail, and each requirement has been carefully considered and the appropriate solution found.

Samuro office furniture.

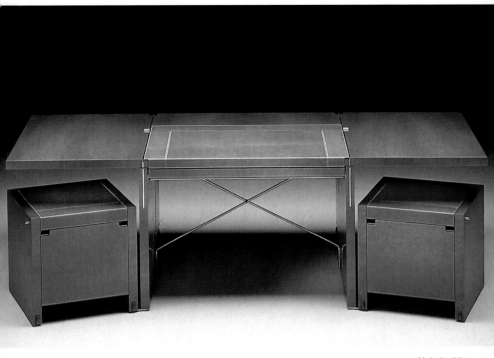

Nobel table.

Paralelas table.

Office filing cabinets.

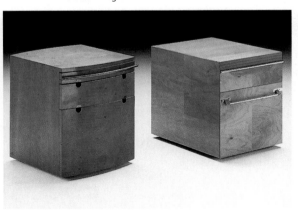

Lamps for the study

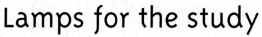

Lamp by Adolf Loos (1910).

Lamp by Josef Hoffmann (1903).

Marie by Jorge Pensi for Blux.

Capalonga (1982) by Tobia Scarpa for Flos.

JL 2P (1997) by Juka Letviska for artek.

Costanza by Paolo Rizzatto for Luceplan.

Open by Josep Magem for Acord Disegno.

Pierrot de Tobia Scarpa para Flos.

Taps by Jorge Pensi for Blux.

HIpotensa (1976) by Achille Castiglioni, for Flos.

Ara by Philippe Starck for Flos.

Tango by Stephen Copeland for Flos.

Ketupa by Josep Lluscà for Blauet.

Titos by Massimo Baldi for Effetto Luce.

Office chairs

Solo. Josep Lluscà.

Sara. Sergi y Oscar Devesa.

Eina. Josep Lluscà.

BCN. Josep Lluscà.

Liona. Gemma Bernal y Ramon Isern.

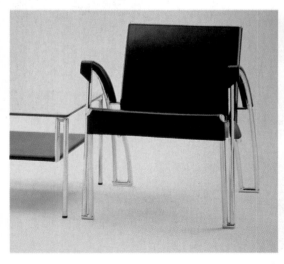

Sillón *Bravo*. Sergi y Oscar Devesa.

Kadira. BD.

Global. Josep Lluscà.

Bulo.

Demo. Calligaris.

Bulo.

Visiteur chair. Bulo.

N.Y. Calligaris.

Convention. Calligaris.

X. Pep Bonet.

Bitmap. Calligaris.

Doble X. Oscar Tusquets.

Bitmap. Calligaris.

Project. Calligaris.

Office tables

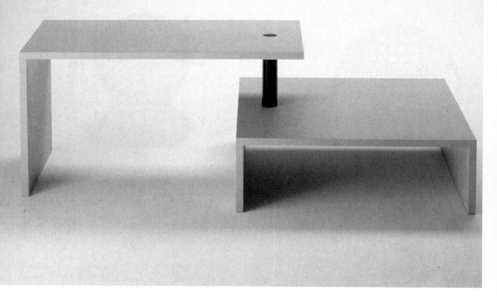

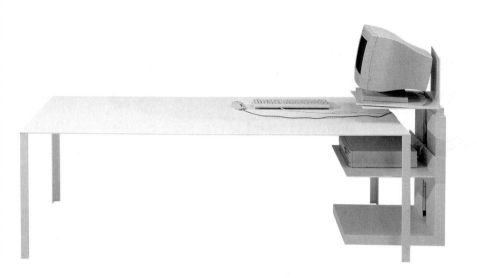

Less. Jean Nouvel.

Basellone. A.Castiglioni.

H2O for Claire – Bulo.

Circular Ten. Gabriel Teixidó

Neutra. Gabriel Teixidó

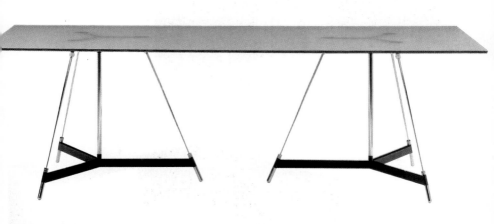

Ten. Gabriel Teixidó

Gazel. Mateo Grassi.

Table with bookcase. Lluis Clotet.

Global. unit. Mario Ruiz.

Global. unit. Mario Ruiz.

Nobel. Jaume Tresserra.

Legend 102. Mateo Grassi

Bedrooms

The bedroom is obviously for sleeping in, but it is also usually used as a place for keeping clothes, getting dressed, and preparing to go out. Some bedrooms even have a special area for working, separate from the relaxation area. In these types of rooms with different spaces, it is vital to choose the right furniture and position it appropriately.

The traditional double bedroom witnesses and reflects the changes in the relationships between men and women resulting from our modern lifestyles, and ideally both halves of a couple should have their own space, well defined and sufficient in size — a separate section each in the closets and on the shelves, for example.

The bed is the vital element in a bedroom, and this means it should be the first piece of furniture to be allocated a space. It should face the door, with the headboard against the wall. This positioning is not arbitrary, for it means that we have the advantage of being able to control access to the room from the bed. In double bedrooms, there should ideally be access to the bed from both sides, and this must be borne in mind when deciding where to put the bed. If there is only a single bed, or twin beds, then they can have one side against the wall. It is best not to put the bed underneath the window. In fact, every effort should be made to keep it clear of the window, to avoid the cold in winter and drafts in summer. If it is put against a wall, this should be an inside wall, as it will be drier and warmer there. Another very practical touch is a shelf to replace the headboard, as all kinds of personal objects can be put there.

Of course, the closet also is also a determining factor when we arrange the furniture. In cases of single beds, it is best to put the closet against the wall at the foot of the bed, so that the two elements are on either side of the room. If there are twin beds, there are greater possibilities of varying the distribution, but there are also greater problems of space. We must choose a closet suited to the room; if not, we shall be in the situation that we have all

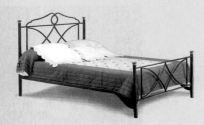

seen on occasion, in which the room is completely dominated by the closet and the visual harmony of the bedroom is completely ruined. If it is decided to build the closet into the wall, then it is important that it goes up to the ceiling; there are few things that unbalance the proportions of a room as much as an ugly hole between the top of a closet and the ceiling — not to mention the fact that it is also an unnecessary loss of space.

We have seen how the bedroom revolves round the bed, with the closet coming next in importance due to its size. Another basic element is the nightstand, or a substitute for it, on which we can put the alarm clock, a book, or the radio. Other important features are a light source and an attractive chair.

Things get more complicated if the bedroom fulfills any additional functions. In some houses it serves as a secondary lounge or work area; and in some homes the furnishing can be extremely comprehensive, including a desk, a couch, armchairs, lamps, furniture for storing a variety of items (folders, files, tapes, a sewing kit), bookshelves, a television, hi-fi equipment, an exercise machine, and so on. The furniture can be as elaborate as we want, depending on our taste and personal habits.

Our decisions on decoration obviously have to take into account the size of the room. Most bedrooms are small, and their layout has to be meticulously planned if we want them to contain anything more than a bed, a small table, space for clothes, and a chair. As a general principle, we must always be aware of how to take the maximum advantage of the space available to us.

The best for a bedroom, in practical terms, is to create specific areas, to find a nook for each function so that they do not get in each other's way, especially if you are going to spend long periods of time in the room. Modern design and new technology can provide wonderful solutions to relieve problems of space: there are multipurpose pieces of furniture, made up of elements that can be combined in different ways as required, and that can be bought separately, which allows us to assemble them in accordance with our own particular needs.

A bathroom in the bedroom

The idea behind incorporating a bathroom into the bedroom is to preserve the feeling of intimacy we associate with both these spaces. On the one hand, the privacy of the combination and, on the other, the comfort make this a perfect solution that turns the bedroom into a unique private area. The coordination of the bedroom and the bathroom can prove extremely attractive if we bear in mind that they are two rooms that can use similar chromatic ranges, and that significant details are of the essence in their decoration.

The bookcase serves as a sliding door that separates the bathroom area from the bedroom.

The blue finish of the sandstone in this bathroom combines with the different shades of the elements in the bedroom.

The glass fittings, the basis of this bathroom's decoration, provide a contrast with the warmth of the tones in the adjoining bedroom.

Coordinating with white

The color white, when present on walls, furniture, and fabrics, is a classic element that adapts to any decorative style by endowing it with greater luminosity. Using white in different textures and finishes is not only visually pleasing but intensifies the aura of restfulness and relaxation necessary in a bedroom.

Blue and white, a classic combination for this bedroom with a slightly naval touch.

This spacious and austere bedroom takes full advantage of the sunlight that pours in through a small window.

A simple space dominated by the bed with a canopy that combines classicism and modernity.

The avant-garde character of this individual bedroom is heightened by a wall dotted with circular mirrors.

The simplicity of the design on the headboard of this bed, and the combination of whites with wood appear to increase the feeling of comfort.

The absence of color in this bedroom is compensated for by the warmth of the wooden floor.

Fabrics for the bedroom

There are a huge variety of fittings suitable for a bedroom. The wealth of materials on the market, the different finishes, and the range of textures, colors, and prints all add up to an infinity of possible combinations.

The traditional elements are cushions, drapes, and bed linen; as well as upholstered headboards, stools, and armchairs. When deciding on the color of these fittings the overall decoration of the bedroom must be taken into account: warm colors combined with wood, classic fabrics in pale colors for traditional bedrooms, and so on.

A combination of cushions that reflects all the tones of this bedroom.

Bed with upholstered headboard. The color of the material matches the ochers and reddish shades in the rest of the room.

Classic look with the headboard cushions upholstered in the same fabric as the stools at the foot of the bed.

This bed, complemented by an original bedside table, reflects all the colors that surround it.

The warmth of this bedroom is accentuated by the shades of reds in the drapes and the large rug.

Romantic style with drapes and upholstery in white to reflect the natural light.

The bay window allows the bed
to overlook the garden.

Next to a window

A window next to the bed
provides another focus for the
room, allowing the sunlight to
filter into the setting and
offering a smoother, more
relaxed look. By putting the
bed in a position where it
overlooks the landscape
outside but does not receive
direct sunlight on the pillows,
contact with the outside world
becomes a determining factor
in improving relaxation.

The paneling that protects the
head of the bed bestows a special
character on this room with
several light sources.

Wedge-shape bedroom in *Villa Zapu*. Its
original structure permits a total
contact with the exterior.

The rooms of this home surround an inner courtyard. The windows facing each other constitute an original and unexpected visual motif.

The horizontal planes of this large window have been exploited by building a wide headboard underneath.

The door leading to the yard is the principle feature of this simple linear bedroom.

Wood in the bedroom

Wood has been adapted to various fashions and styles and is still in demand as a warm and comfortable material. Its traditional use in furnishing has increased with the popularity of parquet and paneling where, far from hiding its natural characteristics, its original tone is emphasized with the application of varnishes and wax. Pale woods of exotic origin, with a flexibility that permits their use in any design, have given rise to simpler and more refined styles.

The interior of a wood cabin, maximum warmth in its minimal expression.

Furniture unit with white front that matches the upholstery of the headboard and the armchair.

Simple and avant-garde forms designed in wood for this bedstead.

The natural tones of the arch leading to the terrace serve as the focus for this classic-style bedroom.

The large headboard structure is the center around which the bed and side tables are organized, creating a space with horizontal continuity made entirely of wood.

The *Jacobsen* chair, the reference point for observing the interplay of the shades of wood.

Metal structures

The classic look of this bed with a canopy blends in perfectly with the trendy style of the bedroom. Design by Pepita Teixidó and Xavier Sust.

Metal bed structures have also evolved towards more contemporary concepts. Simpler designs, combining other materials and involving painting the metal in various colors, have revitalized this type of bedroom, although the classic touch is still present in the adornment used in the majority of designs.

Cleopâtre model in blue for Roche & Bobois. Touches of color on metal beds allow them to fit in more easily in any setting.

Models by Cantari.

Two single beds joined together
make up this original design, made
of metal combined with
wickerwork. *Mezzaluna* for Cantari.

Lexington bed
with canopy.
From Potterybarn.

A simple wooden bar is used
to update the traditional bed
with rungs. *Geo*, from Cantari.

Detail of the ornamentation at the foot of the bed. *Ambra* model from Cantari.

Ambra model from Cantari. Discreet ornamentation, with porcelain finishing, bestows a simple elegance on the setting.

Mezzaluna model with the two beds separated.

In the romantic style

The romantic style uses pieces of classic furniture but does not stick to any rigid guidelines. It combines antique furniture with drapes and fabrics to give the former new tones and finishes, and borrows elements from rustic styles like the Provençal to endow the bedroom with a touch of rural classicism.

Double bedroom in the Provençal style. The color on the wall has been carefully chosen to achieve a better match with the pale tones of the furniture and accessories.

The romantic dormitory, unlike the strictly classical one, embraces modern elements like simple halogen lamps.

The sharp whiteness of the upholstery makes a dramatic contrast with the walls and drapes in this bedroom.

The duality created by the
dark wood and the white
materials is echoed in the
painted wallpaper.

This combination from KA International does not commit itself to any classic style. It asserts its own personality by making color the dominant feature.

A stylish element can imbue the whole bedroom with a special romantic character. The wicker chair and the sheets with white stripes are two details that provide a calculated visual impact.

An oriental influence

This bed is set next to a window on a wooden tatami. The special warmth of the materials gives the setting an atmosphere redolent of comfort and security.

The creation of a space in which the lines are allowed to flow without any interruption results in the concept of the bedroom stripped down to its purest expression. Restfulness is the main aim of a decoration in which the minimal presence of objects lends harmony to the setting in order to relax the senses. Floral ornamentation, tatamis, and futons are other options in a decorative style based on a particular philosophy of comfort.

The simplicity of a mattress on the floor contrasts with the strength of the wood in an architectural setting. Anderson & Schwartz.

The traditional paper door creates an interesting play of light on the natural tones of this design by A. Sakamoto for the *Hakuei Residence*.

The purity of form and
decorative simplicity that define
the oriental style give this space
its distinctive character. *Casa
Bergadà*, Tonet Sunyer.

With the bed flanked by a tea table and facing the window, this bedroom seems to convert relaxation and sleep into a mystical exercise.

The search for maximum simplicity has led to the architectural elements remaining exposed, thereby dictating the structure of the interior decoration. *Blades House*, California.

Design with a minimum of intervention

The criteria for good design are often contradictory, but one thing they all have in common is simplicity: a minimum of intervention, the constant search for the utmost simplicity of line and form so that a design is self-explanatory and, therefore, easily comprehensible. Luminous spaces, pale colors, and furniture stripped down to its basic structure, without any superfluous adornment, are the basic characteristic of bedrooms created solely for sleeping in.

The large windows and imposing beam, a reminder of the original industrial function of the space, are more than enough to decorate this bedroom.

The headboard has a slight curve, making it both functional and more comfortable.

The functional look of this closet, running parallel to the wall, suggests a large inner capacity and seeks to take the maximum advantage of the available space.

The line proposed by Galli for
a bedroom entirely created for
the nighttime. The duality of
the wooden tones and the
white creates a relaxing and
luminous space.

The simplicity derived from the absence of furniture is the dominant feature of this space.

The minimalist lines endow this design by Piero Lissoni with a very individual yet timeless quality.

The main bedroom of the *Lawson-West House*, designed by Eric Owen Moss, is dominated by a long opening in the ceiling providing a very dramatic effect.

The panel is made with a cedar veneer finished off with varnish. The simplicity of *Little Nemo* by Mireia Riera bases the entire decoration on this stark element.

Jordi Romeu is responsible for this design, called *Lolita*. Simplicity and practicality in a headboard fixed to the wall.

At the foot of the bed

The versatility of elements in wood and metal placed at the foot of the bed has made them an ever more popular addition to bedrooms, as they not only provide comfort but are also visually attractive. Their strategic situation makes them a highlight of the room.

Combination created by Laura Ashley. The presence of the upholstered stool emphasizes the romantic personality of the setting.

The metal structure of the seats, in the same style as the bedside tables, provide touches of modernity in this elegant bedroom.

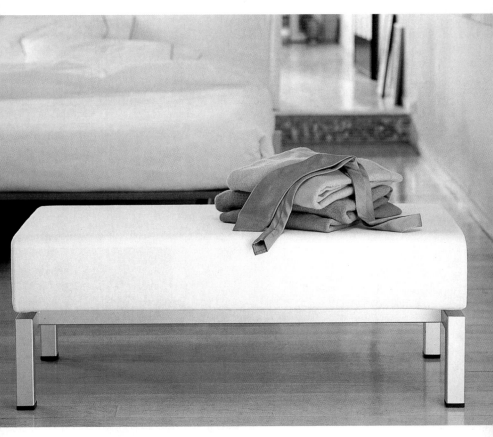

Small bench upholstered in
white, situated near the bed to
be more practical.

Estambul divan from KA International. Taken out of the context of the setting, it is apparent that the upholstery totally dictates the personality of this dramatic element.

Combination in blue and white from KA International. The classic structure of the divan contrasts with the more modern upholstery.

Coordinated in three basic tones – wood, white, and gray – this ensemble from KA International gives a very spacious and refined look to the bedroom.

A perfect display

These dressing rooms have been
created according to purely
esthetic criteria, and their
visual impact is derived from a
thorough planning of the
details, the furniture, and the
lighting. Low tables, display
units, and the odd chair allow
clothes to continue expressing
their personality even when
they are not being worn.

This combination from
Porada expertly balances
storage and esthetics
without sacrificing any of
its great capacity.

The versatility of low pieces of furniture
permits the arrangement of the dressing
room to suit any requirement and also
the display of various accessories.

Without any need to have all
the clothes on show, the light
picks out parts of the dressing
room and turns them into a
distinctive showcase.

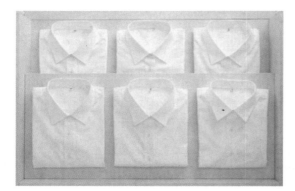

Storage units like drawers and clothes rails, created from the perspective of visual display. Tissetanto.

The personal taste for a single chromatic range in clothing turns this dressing room into an exercise in simple forms and gives it a refined look.

The installation of shelves and
clothes rails covers all the
practical requirements while
giving the dressing room a
dramatic visual impact.

Large dressing rooms

**These spaces, created to store
clothes and accessories, have been
turned into one enormous closet. As
they occupy an area separate from
the bedroom itself, they offer a
chance to put in seats, mirrors, and
other elements that increase
comfort and endow their
surroundings with personality.**

Night Mobil
combination by Girgi.
The dark wood of
the drawers is
complemented by the
paler tone of the boxes
– an attractive way to
avoid overloading the
well-utilized space.

Putting all the storage
elements against the walls
creates a central space
appropriate for seats and small
pieces of furniture.

Luminosity is extremely important in this combination by Tisettanto. A dressing room revolving around the colors and textures of the clothes.

Small details take on importance in the structuring of this combination around the central bench.

Close-up of a drawer designed to hang trousers. This type of solution combines visual appeal with practical requirements to brighten up an interior.

A dressing room in the closet

The size of the closet provides a comfortable space for dressing, based on the structure of the closet itself. The internal organization of these dressing rooms, the majority set into a corner of the bedroom, often allows for a seat or small piece of furniture, giving the interior a style of its own.

Small spaces need good inner distribution if they are not to lose their practical function.

This combination with a very austere appearance, from the *Space* collection by Move, hints at the nature of the dressing room through frosted glass windows.

By treating the dressing room as an integral part of the bedroom, the feeling of transition between the two spaces is erased because the dressing room seems to take on the appearance of an external closet.

Dressing room from Besana, built into the corner of a closet from the same collection. The pale colors heighten the impression received of luminosity.

Dressing room closet from the *Proteo* series from Vibrio. A sober combination made of dark woods that contrast with the pale finish of the interior.

The simplicity of the design and finishings in this combination for Move integrates the austere interior with the minimalist style of the bedroom.

A roomy walk-in closet.

Closets with transparent doors

The visual possibilities offered by transparent glass doors rescue the closet from the traditional image of a somber square. Treatment with acid and combinations with color and wood create new ways to coordinate the closet with the other elements of the bedroom.

Morgante I collection by the Italian designer Paolo Piva. The modules of this ensemble permit variations in the combinations of wood and glass and make it totally adaptable to any wall.

This closet, which creates a large inner space for clothes, bases its structure on the architecture of the bedroom. Its limits are marked by doors with glass that has been treated with acid.

The character of this model designed by Dell'Orto, which is totally transparent and has intelligent interior lighting, is entirely derived from the simple and geometrical lines.

By combining white with the
shadowy effect of the glass, this
design from the *Levante* collection
of the Mobil Girgi company gives
a totally minimalist finish.

Closet made in aluminum and
Millepunti glass by the Move
company. It is completely
integrated into the wall, but in
appearance it resembles a door to
a terrace.

Drive series from
Besana. The
upholstered bench
placed in front of
this closet seeks
to give the
impression of a
suite. The closet
combines shades
of cream and
brown to achieve
a simple finish.

Fronts in white

For esthetic and practical reasons, the choice of white for the front part of a closet is one way of subduing its visual impact. This type of finish fits in perfectly in any setting, even the most minimalist ones.

A glimpse inside this closet from the Poliform company reveals the distinctive structure of the sliding doors, with their concealed tracking system.

The practical look of this closet, which runs along a wall, gives the suggestion of a great *interior* capacity.

Poliform offers this closet
made of large white panels
with natural wood edges.

The versatility of this design from the *Todi* series for the Mobil Girgi company gives rise to a space structured around an in-built closet, which finishes off its exterior design with the rectangular shapes of windows.

Distinctive design from Irene Puorto for the *Oceano* series from the Galli company. The purity of the lines and the simplicity of the chromatic range turn this piece of furniture into an exercise in both style and functionality.

Another design from Irene Puorto for the *Oceano* series from the Galli company.

Interior view of
the *XL* series by
Tisettanta.

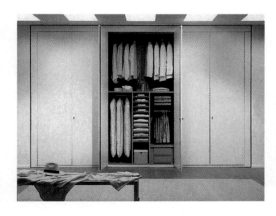

Quotidiano collection
from Mobil Girgi. A
stark interior design
emphasizes the
functional nature of
this austere unit, made
all in white.

Closet from the *XL* series by Tisettanta. The simplicity of the three white panels gives this closet a distinctive look, and the design of the inset-style handle provides a finish of great elegance.

Close-up of a handle, with simple forms and natural tones.

The fashion designer Toni Miró is the inspiration for this closet designed by Pep Bonet. The doors are replaced by drapes in the form of quadrants, thus creating a very refined finish.

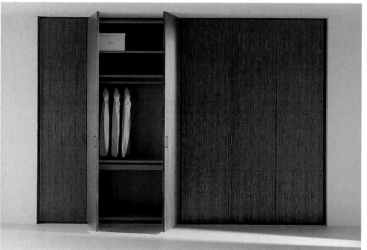

This model from the *Sistema* system created by the Brivio company reduces details to the minimum and seems to be a continuation of the wall made of wood.

Updating a classic

The idea of the closet as an element for containing clothes and, therefore, a heavy structure deposited in the bedroom that determines the decoration has changed. The style now is a model of discretion, which demands that closets blend visually with the rest of the elements in the bedroom. A scarcity of details and designs in straight lines turn the closet into an extension of the wall that it is set against, and as a result it has become a visually elegant and muted piece of furniture.

Levante series from Mobil Girgi. The horizontal planes suggested by the natural grain of the wood contrast with the vertical lines of the closet to give a more balanced look.

FTS Fortuna model made out of natural wood and metal. The original lighting system confers a halogen lamp on each double door of the closet.

The classic lines of this closet are almost architectural and suggest a rational organization on the inside.

Storage space under the mattress

Versatility in any element in the bedroom is translated into a rational use of space. This criterion has led to bed designs with a structure allowing all the space taken up by beds to be taken advantage of. Without making any visual concessions, these beds are examples of both practicality and comfort. They will not be used to their full extent unless there is easy access to their interior.

Todi model from Mobil Girgi. Versatility is complemented by simplicity in this updating of the romantic metal bed.

A view of the *Tristano* model by Poliform opened. Dead or inaccessible areas are avoided by opening from the top of the bed.

Poliform followed some very simple esthetic criteria to make the *Tristano* bed. Its finishing hides the system that closes the space underneath and so completely conceals the structure's double function.

Twin beds

The spare bedroom, normally reserved for guests, is usually laid out along functional lines. Stylish details are the basis of a discreet decoration and a visual look revolving round comfort.

This combination provides an original solution to the problem of catering for the various possible relationships between the occupants of the beds. The same combination with the beds together: the mobile structure includes the headboard, which also serves as a sliding door that hides the shelf – it will no longer serve as a bedside table.

Above: Double bed from the *Duplex* series, made with elliptical laminated steel tubing. Design by Gabriel Teixidó for Enea.

Top: A modern combination that sets off the white of the bed structure with the cherrywood color used for the side tables. Ensemble from the *Art* series by the Italian company Galli.

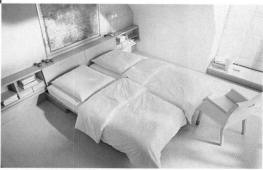

Two large classic beds made of metal contrast with the simplicity of the lines of the room, which set off their very distinctive romantic character.

Original solutions

These dressing areas, with their visual austerity and simple forms, are outstanding on account of their creation of spaces that revolve around a piece of furniture or architectural element without any need to completely set their boundaries. These settings, with a character and originality all their own, make it possible to install a dressing room with a great visual impact within the bedroom itself.

G. V. Plazzogna is responsible for this design for the Galli company. The striking design of the headboard complements a versatile bedside table.

The idea of a headboard stuck on a wall creates the impression that the bedroom and dressing room are in two independent areas. Design by Alvaro Guarro for Matías Guarro.

A partition separates the bedroom from the dressing area in this Barcelona attic designed by Pere Cortacans.

This design, based on the
architectural structure of the
bedroom, turns the whole
room into a spacious
dressing room.

The structure of this dressing
room, in the form of a corridor, is
emphasized with the original
touch of a classic piece of
antique furniture to serve as a
chest of drawers.

Children's bedrooms

Children's bedrooms will go through changes as their occupants grow up, and for this reason it is important to provide them with furniture that is flexible enough to answer their needs over a period of several years. It is clear, then, that we must have a vision of the future when we come to decorate and furnish a child's bedroom.

Whereas the parents themselves can be entirely responsible for the decoration of a baby's room, as children grow we must allow them to become increasingly involved in the layout of the room. As they are going to spend many hours there it is vital that they feel at home in it.

The essential elements of a baby's room are the crib, the dressing table, and an element for changing the baby. It is best not to overload a baby's room with too many things, unless there is a large budget available, as they will become redundant once the baby has grown.

When the child reaches preschool age his or her room will undergo various changes. If the room has to be used both for sleeping and for playing, as is normally the case, every inch takes on vital importance. Everything will be much more orderly if there is enough space to store books and toys. One possible solution for toys is boxes, if possible with compartments, that can also serve as seats. As for books, classic bookcases are the most appropriate option, but we must make sure that the child can reach them. However, in any event we must forsake the notion of a completely tidy children's room.

If we put in a closet for clothes, it is best to get a tall one, since it will last longer than one that is made specifically for children. We can also add a chest of drawers for certain items of clothing like socks and T-shirts. Bunks are the ideal choice of bed for older children. What is more, they are an excellent means of saving space, especially if there are two children who have to sleep in a small bedroom.

A room for adolescents must contain not only a sleeping area but also a space for studying, listening to music, or chatting with friends. It is advisable to define these two areas clearly by arranging the furniture suitably, and by introducing different decorative effects. It is a good idea to let young people participate in the decoration, or at least offer them a range of possibilities, so that they feel that it is they themselves who have made the final decision. Obviously, adolescents need a bed, with perhaps an extra one for putting up friends; but they also require a work table big enough for a computer, at least one chair, a space suitable for a music system, and storage space; as well as anything else demanded by their personal tastes and needs.

When considering the floor and walls, we must let our common sense guide us, whether in rooms for toddlers or for older children. The floor must be comfortable for crawling, and later for sitting and playing for long stretches. Carpets are not practical because, although they are very attractive, they get dirty very quickly.

The walls can be either papered or painted, but in either case they must be easy to wash. We have to bear in mind that children are constantly scraping their toys against the walls or scribbling on them. Ideally, we should be prepared to apply a new coat of paint from time to time, and if we prefer wallpaper we must make sure it is washable.

Good lighting is also crucial. Our lighting requirements will inevitably change as the child grows up. Environmental lighting, whether from a central light or wall lamps, is indispensable. A desk lamp is also necessary, especially if the child has a work table, and another light should be placed on the bedside table so that he or she can read in bed. If the room has the benefit of natural lighting, that is perfect as children will appreciate the cheerfulness afforded by sunlight, just as they will be grateful if they are not allocated the smallest room in the home. With the passing of the years the functions of the room will increase and, as a result, so will the need for additional space.

For new arrivals

The baby's room can acquire a delicate yet functional atmosphere in which ideas about furniture take on new meanings. Visual appeal and safety are indispensable for the creation of a relaxed and secure environment.

Design by KA International combining blue and white. The classic metal structure of the crib stands out in this equally classic setting.

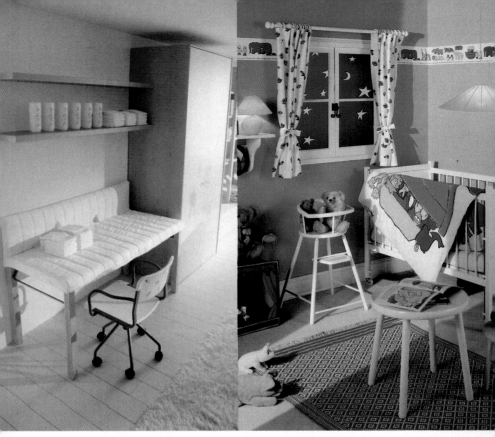

Baby changer from the *Maxim* series by Galli. The wood and fabric structure takes the form of a desk to achieve the maximum comfort and functionality, without sacrificing any visual appeal.

An entertaining room for a baby. The organization of the space in a child's bedroom is subject to constant changes that give rise to functional decorative solutions.

Opposite and right: *Leo* crib, designed by Irene Puorto. The original wooden structure conveys an impression of rational functionality combined with a refined visual impact.

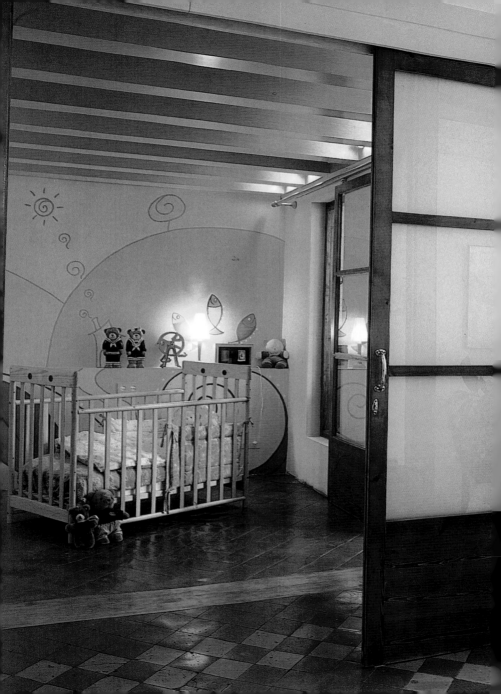

Interior of a modern children's bedroom. Some unusual elements are distinguished by their simplicity and functionality.

Antique rustic shapes define this children's room. The meeting points of the beams and the walls create an original ledge, which is decorated with toys.

A practical bedroom and playing space has been set up in one part of the home on one side of the sliding doors.

Sweet and feminine

Bedrooms for girls, full of details that define their decoration, conjure up a world with elements that can change very abruptly. Classic elements, with their special way of interpreting elegance, are finished with soothing colors to create a highly personal and intimate atmosphere.

Daisy Rose ensemble in pink and white. A classic combination of colors for a very feminine bedroom.

Wallpaper and drapes from the *Ballet* series by Laura Ashley. The themes in the decoration of girls' bedrooms often includes elements with which they can easily identify.

Details and subtleties are the dominant features of girls' bedrooms.

Catch-all closets

The closet, the most static element in a bedroom, can discreetly and practically follow the form of the wall and so leave more space in the center of the room.

The closet's double function, as a storage space for both toys and clothes, means that it can have a complicated internal organization, with one area for the child and another for the mother, and very different layouts in each one.

Combination made of wood lacquered in blue and green. The closet appears as an individual element that divides the room into two separate areas.

Tall closet made of solid pine stained blue and finished with fabric. The simple look of this piece gives it a very romantic air.

One classic way of gaining more space is that of putting a closet unit above the bed. This composition by Battistella achieves a simple and refined look by combining wood with pale colors.

Battistella is responsible for this pale-colored closet unit. The practicality of these type of elements, going from wall to wall, is complemented by its strong visual impact.

The form of this closet in the corner of the room aims to hold as much as possible whilst also taking advantage of dead spaces.

Maximum capacity in a composition by Battistella that creates a bookcase structure out of the form of the closet.

Sleeping and studying

Older children's bedrooms are used for several activities, each of which require their own space and furniture. The bed is the biggest and most important element, but it also needs a desk. The study area must be self-contained, well lit, and provided with eleménts that are both functional and comfortable. The importance of this work area has given rise to some very intelligent designs, which marry maximum versatility with a very dynamic visual impact.

Original desk made entirely of wood. Its functional structure is complemented by a very refined look.

An extremely functional and visually striking desk, made of steel and wood.

Functional blue desk. The vertical bookshelf provides a space for books without overloading the limited space.

Desk designed around a raised bed. The curved top increases the work space and adds visual charm.

The versatility of this desk means that it can be stored above the chest of drawers, or folded out into the room when it is being used.

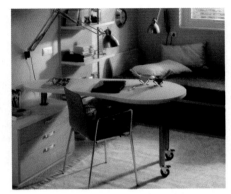

Original and versatile desk. The structure of the table helps to take full advantage of the space by incorporating a chest of drawers under the retractable worktop.

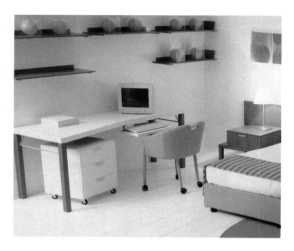

The *Argento Vivo* unit offers a look based on highly functional minimalist lines. The wood is complemented by pale colors that brighten up the work space.

The structure of this bedroom makes it possible to put a classic-style table under the window. This arrangement is very popular, on account of the importance of natural light in the study area.

Desk with bookcase placed under a window. The classic lines of the furniture evoke a sobriety that encourages serious study.

Traditional layout for a bedroom, with the work area parallel to the bed. The versatile bookcase demonstrates its utility for the desk whilst also serving as a bedside unit.

Forms stripped down to basics for a desk from the Galli company. The simple lines and absence of superfluous elements create a special clarity, highly suited to study.

A functional but relaxed style from Mobil Girgi. The study elements create two independent areas, one with a retractable table and the other with a piece of furniture designed especially for a computer.

First maturity

By combining a relaxed decoration with a new sobriety in search of its own definition of elegance, the older child's bedroom presents a series of contrasts that indicate a change in mentality and a more rational approach. There is no longer any attempt to find a uniform decorative style; instead, the room becomes a living space full of details that reflect the character of the occupant.

The shapes in the bedroom start to become more discreet, even though they still conform to a relaxed and carefree style, albeit trying to adapt to the demands of a new lifestyle.

A nest bed made of elliptical laminated steel tubing. The *Duplex* model, designed by Gabriel Teixidó for Enea, uses its sophisticated simplicity to fit into any setting.

Simplicity and comfort in a setting that combines wood and natural fibers to achieve an effect of well ordered informality.

Raised beds

Children's bedrooms are often shared spaces that serve more than one function. One area for playing, another for studying, and yet another for sleeping will have to be multiplied by two if children share a room, leading to restrictions on space that require solutions of the utmost practicality and, on occasions, tact.

Raised beds are cheerful and practical elements that make it possible to take full advantage of space without losing any visual attraction. New designs and modern combinations that move the bed break the image of the classic bunk and create spaces for closets or studies. They make the raised bed the best solution for bedrooms for more than one child.

Two mobile raised beds that can be moved and fitted together, providing an opportunity to increase the space available in the bedroom. Originality and practicality in a combination of simple forms and refined lines.

Functionality and visual charm in a combination of structural simplicity that takes advantage of the corner of the room and creates an enclosed space for sleeping.

A very functional combination from Battistella. By moving the top bed to one side, a space is created beneath for a low closet.

The space created by raising the bed is used by a low but deep closet, suitable for hanging clothes.

Gutvik model from Ikea. The classic bunk structure is made of untreated pinewood.

Raised bed that moves along a track on the wall to cover either the other bed or the desk. The functionality of these mobile elements embraces both originality and visual appeal.

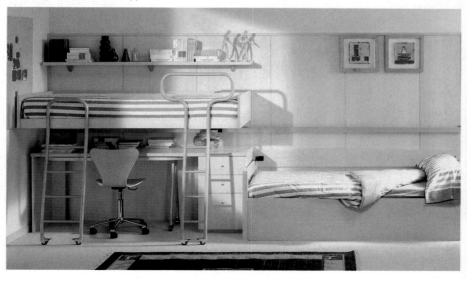

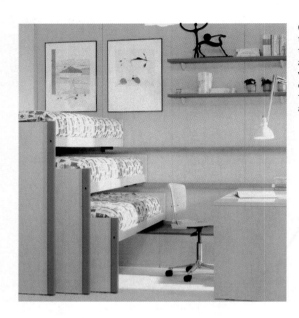

Combination of three raised beds that fit into one another. The versatility of these elements means that the sleeping area is also suited to study.

This combination by Besana provides the lower bed and desk with rails that allow them to be moved simply.

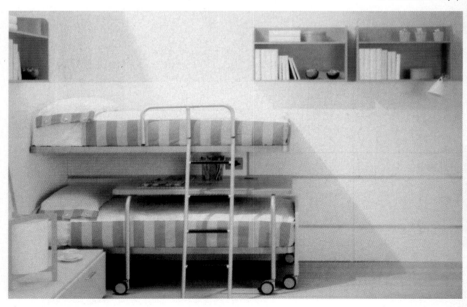

Minisprazio combination by Sangiorgio. The staircase at the back is both practical and original, as every step contains a storage box.

Romantic combination of raised bed and couch-bed. The height of the bed and the solidity of the ladder create the impression of two independent floors.

 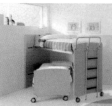 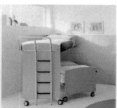 

An illustration of the versatility of the *Gulliver* model by Besana. The variety of combinations that can be adopted by this unit endows it with both dynamism and charm.

The simple forms of Besana's *Gulliver* model combine versatility and elegance without overpowering the limited space.

An interpretation of the static bunk by Mobil Girgi. The straight lines and functional design make this combination not only practical but also lively.

Bedrooms for young people

A young person's bedroom is a space that looks to the future, and it is subject to the most typical requirements of the contemporary environment, as both children and adolescents must live today to the full to reap the benefits of tomorrow. The ideas shown here are top-quality designs that answer to the demand for greater definition in spaces for young people.

The bed and complementary furnishing are tucked into the space formed by storage units to one side and above.

The *Woodline* collection by San Giorgio includes simple, versatile models that give a setting a very youthful look.

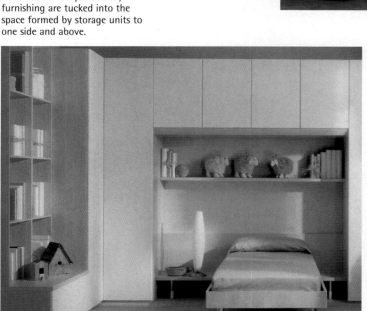

Ideal study unit for children. Furniture with casters, and combinations with the matching table flap and closets.

Two sharply contrasting alternatives: a
country setting and a naval one.

Bathrooms

Generally speaking, we do not indulge in much leisure activity in the bathroom. However, we all have experience of that everyday scene in which various members of the family want to use this room at the same time. There is no doubt that it is an indispensable part of any home, but it is also within our range of possibilities to convert this functional space into a haven of relaxation and enjoyment.

At the beginning of the twentieth century everything connected with the bathroom was treated with reticence, but these days it does not remain in the shadows. In fact, it has become a status symbol and a mark of personal style, as people try to turn their bathroom into an area that is both comfortable and visually attractive. It is only in a pleasant space of this kind that, imbued with a certain Roman spirit, we can wallow in a foamy bath not merely for hygienic reasons but also for pure pleasure.

The bathroom is usually small and deprived of natural light. This means that the distribution of its elements and the appropriate lighting must be considered with great care. Essentially, the layout of the space must respond to our needs and personal tastes.

The most convenient position for the bathtub is at the back of the room, or in the center if space permits, with the bidet and the toilet on the same wall as the entrance, to avoid making them the focal point of the bathroom. It is also important that the sink is at the right height — normally 3 feet (1 m) from the floor. It is also possible to install low sinks for children, but this is nothing more than a whim as the children will soon outgrow them.

Moreover, to make the most of this space we have to ask ourselves several questions: whether the bathroom is going to be the only one in the house, how many people are going to use it, and what it is going to be used for. If it is only for one or two people, then it does not need to be very spacious, and neither does it need big closets, as shelves will be sufficient to maintain the minimum of order.

In a very busy bathroom, on the other hand, size is of paramount importance. If our budget permits, it is very useful to divide the bathroom into compartments, thus separating the toilet and bidet from the rest of the fittings. In this way, one member of the family can be using the toilet or bidet whilst another is leisurely taking a shower or brushing his or her teeth.

The most luxurious bathrooms also tend to house two distinct spaces. One pays homage to the cult of hygiene and relaxation, with its hydromassage bathtub or shower booth with steam bath. The other caters for the cult of the body beautiful in the more esthetic sense, being devoted to cosmetics, exercise, or an artificial sunbed — a treat for both body and soul. In this way many pleasure-seekers turn their bathroom into a room in its own right.

As regards the lighting, there are two possibilities: to create an intense light or a smoother, more muted one. If you do not want to commit yourself to either of these alternatives, you can put in a dimmer switch, which permits a whole range of variations. In any event, an intense brilliant white light increases the impression of size, and, in this respect, incandescent light sources in the ceiling and a few strategically placed mirrors give that illusion of luminosity that so many people look for in their bathroom.

Another feature that enhances the impression of size in a bathroom is color. Obviously white on a wall, or on a few tiles, reflects light. The cheapest decoration is painting, which offers us a whole host of possibilities: we can have the metal fittings a different color from the walls, giving the bathroom a touch of vitality. Another alternative is wallpaper, although conventional paper must be protected with a special varnish to extend its life, as any mishap, such as splashes of water, can ruin it. It must be added that, in order to eliminate steam from the bathroom, it is necessary to install a window with access to the outside, or, if this is not possible, a skylight or extractor.

As the modern bathroom requires transparency and light, it also therefore demands new materials. Large glass surfaces, mirrors, and partitions are popular, as are walls and floors fitted out in tiles, marble, granite, and parquet. The furnishings feature wood, steel, and glass. Different styles and materials are combined to achieve not only an avant-garde style but also an oasis of luxury and relaxation.

Distributing space

Whether we divide the bathroom into separate independent spaces (toilet, sink, shower area) or incorporate it into the bedroom, separating it with just a transparent glass partition, the distribution of the spaces for the various activities undertaken requires the intimacy of each one to be carefully assessed.

Closing off the toilet and bidet area on the one hand offers a greater freedom for the rest of the bathroom and on the other allows the room to be used by two people at the same time without impinging on privacy.

Two examples of sinks enclosed by transparent glass: the first belongs to an attic designed by Rüdiger Lainer in the Seilergasse in Vienna, the second to a rural house refurbished by BDM Arquitectos on the Spanish Costa Brava.

Opposite: The sink does not necessarily have to be associated with the other activities in the bathroom. Here its placement in an open room has determined the choice of a model in wood and stainless steel designed by Capilla & Vallejo for Rapsel in 1995.

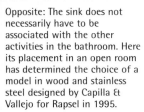

The use of translucent glass allows bathrooms to be lit even with big windows without suffering the inconveniences of total transparency.

Estanislao Pérez Pita has opted for blocks of translucent glass to close off the wall behind the sink. A simple system of rotating axes allows one of the blocks to open for ventilation.

The bathroom in the *Häusler House* by Baumschlager & Eberle is lit by a skylight.

Bathroom light

Bathrooms often dispense with sunlight, either to ensure privacy or to sacrifice this asset in favor of other rooms in the home. Although none of the bathrooms in the following pages has a direct visual relationship with the exterior, daylight nevertheless undoubtedly enhances the atmosphere of each.

Wendell Burnette, in his house in Phoenix, and Alfred Mukenberg, in a London apartment, have both placed a mirror in front of the sink instead of the window.

Simplifying a faucet down to the bare essentials means turning it into a mere pipe. This involves separating the handle from the plumbing by building the mechanisms into the wall. This was the process responsible for some models designed by Jacobsen for Vola (in the photo), and for the *Tara* (Dornbracht), *Axor* (Hansgrohe) and *Minimal* (Boffi) series.

The *Minimal* series of faucets is designed by Giulio Gianturco for Boffi. It was the first time that type-316-L stainless steel was used.

Absolute simplicity

The absolute simplicity
and rigor distinguishing
the design of some
modern bathrooms reflects
the current trend of
incorporating minimalism
into these settings.

Beach chair designed by Povl Bjerregaard for TRIP/TRAP, Scandi Möbler. It is made of teak, and when fully extended it measures 79 x 29 x 13 inches (202 x 73.5 x 32 cm).

The bathroom in the *Price-O'Reilly House*, designed by the architectural couple from Australia Engelen & Moore, is characterized by the profusion of glass elements and mirrors.

The German architect Wolfgang Döring has incorporated an industrial stainless steel sink into the bathroom of the *Stampfel House*. It is fixed to a wall of medium height, which means that no mirror can be hung on it.

Playing with color

There is a certain tradition that demands a total sterile whiteness in bathrooms. However, bathrooms have not always been white and there is no overriding reason for them to be so now. The introduction of a color can transform the appearance of a room which, due to its restricted size, leaves little scope to the imagination.

Friezes are a common device in tiled bathrooms, and the tile manufacturers themselves include several models in their catalogs. In this case the tiles are designed by Pada Lenti for Appiani. The sink is by Philippe Starck for Duravit.

In this bathroom the play with color in the tiles does not spring from the addition of friezes or designs, but from the replacement of some white tiles by ones in different colors. This design has thus been created by the occupant, in accordance with his or her personal tastes and intuition.

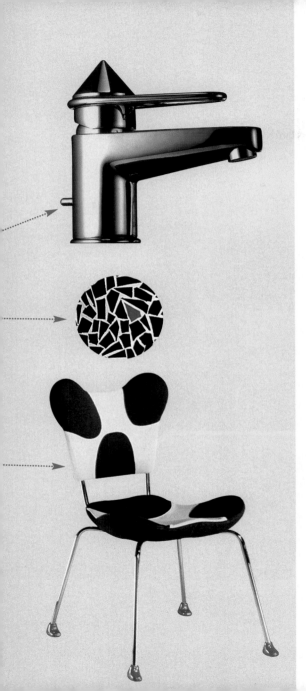

Faucet from the *Point* series designed by Dieter Sieger for the Dornbracht company. The entire series, which also includes accessories like towel rails, shelves, glass holders, soap dishes, and toilet paper holders, is instantly recognizable because all the pipes are crowned by a conical hat.

The *trencadis* technique invented by Antoni Gaudí for his famous buildings in Barcelona consists of smashing tiles and then covering the walls with the resulting fragments. The final appearance presents an array of joins pointing in all directions. It is without doubt a technique highly suited to curved forms, and this was surely the attraction for him.

In 1995 Javier Mariscal created a series of chairs, armchairs, and couches for the Italian company Moroso under the name of *Amorous Furniture*, with clear references to the world of comics – which has great affinities with Mariscal's own creative universe. This is the *Ettorina* chair, with a chromed steel structure and an inflammable polyurethane foam seat.

Sinks in wood

Although the idea of a wooden sink or bathtub still gives us a jolt, if wood is treated in the appropriate manner it is as valid as any other material for making bathroom fittings.

Bathtub in a London apartment refurbished by Simon Conder in 1995.

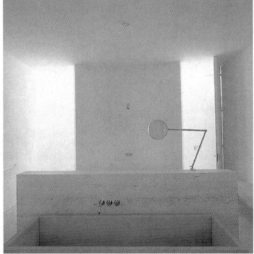

Like Conder, John Pawson comes from a generation of minimalist English architects who have reclaimed wood as a material for sinks and bathtubs. These pieces were specially designed for the *Neuendorf Villa* in Majorca.

The Italian company Agape
produces some exquisite
models of sinks in wood.
Flat is a design by
Giampaolo Benedini.

El Gabbiano, also by
Agape, is designed by
Giuseppe Pascuali, who
is also responsible for
the *351* mirror.

In several scenes in Peter Greenaway's movie "The Belly of the Architect," the main character washed himself in a freestanding bathtub on legs set in the middle of a huge living room. The director obviously sought to convert the act of ablution into a metaphorical ceremony. The movie went on to exert a considerable influence and led to a rediscovery of this kind of bathtub.

Freestanding bathtubs

In contrast with in-built bathtubs, a freestanding one causes great problems for taking a shower without splashing water, as it is almost impossible to protect the bathtub with a curtain.

The nostalgic character of freestanding bathtubs often leads to the installation of period faucets. However, it is also possible to build freestanding bathtubs along modern abstract lines.

The installation of a sunken bath often involves raising the floor by several inches and building one or two steps to compensate.

The construction of a square platform to frame a round bathtub has created a virtually independent space given over to bathing, within the confines of the room.

In this case, the bath enjoys an exceptional position, not far from the bed and facing a window overlooking the yard.

This bath is built into the wall. It has been suitably waterproofed and then covered with colorful mosaic.

Sunker

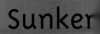

Sunken ba
the bath
take full

Nostalgic bathrooms

The classic
style is popular
today as an
alternative to
minimalism.

In this bathroom in a house in
San Bernabé, in Mexico City,
architects S. Puente and
A. Drewes have succeeded in
creating a decadent atmosphere
by matching the fittings with
the gray marble of the walls.

Most manufacturers of
bathroom fittings include
period-style series in their
catalogs, which means
that it is not necessary to
buy antiques.

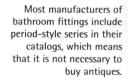

The latest trends point to a return to classic bathrooms, with sinks on pedestals, encaustic tiles, and Art Deco forms as their distinguishing features.

In the last fifteen years the popular French designer Philippe Starck has designed a good number of elements for the bathroom, in collaboration with firms like Duravit (toilet fittings), Hansgrohe (faucets and accessories), Hoesch (bathtubs), Rapsel (sinks), and Fluocaril (toothbrushes).

Lola Herzburg model for Rapsel, with a freestanding support and a sink.

This faucet is part of Hansgrohe's *Axor* series, which also includes built-in faucets, towel rails, mirrors, shelves, soap dishes, clothes hooks, and all kinds of other accessories. The piece of furniture comes from Duravit. It is available in several sizes and the structure is made either in wood or in metal.

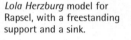

Left and opposite: The Duravit series includes not only built-in sinks but also other forms of raised models.

Starck's choi

Toilet fittings

Forms evolve over time, and what were once conceived for a purely functional intimacy have now become exercises in style. Today's designs for toilet fittings stress the cleanliness and simplicity of the lines to create elements with a distinctive decorative character that do not lose sight of their original practical purpose.

The luminosity of these white toilet fittings contrasts with the colors of the walls and floor in this combination by Laconda.

The idea of putting the toilet elements directly against the wall, thus leaving the floor clear of any obstacles, is a very functional as well as elegant solution.

The pure forms and geometrical interplay of this combination enhance the impression of cleanliness derived from the finishings.

The overall effect in this combination by Villeroy & Boch ensures that light is present in all the details.

Suite by Caro with more rectangular shapes, suggesting an approach to design that shies away from convention.

Close-up of the toilet seat from the *Century Titanic* collection by Villeroy & Boch.

Veranda series from the Roca company. The absence of any straight lines in this ensemble of toilet fittings contrasts with the geometrical combination of the tiles and other elements.

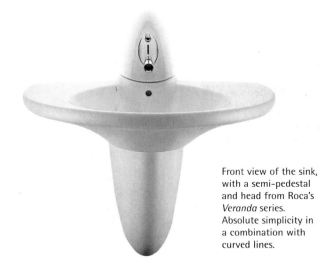

Front view of the sink, with a semi-pedestal and head from Roca's *Veranda* series. Absolute simplicity in a combination with curved lines.

Century Garden collection from Villeroy & Boch. A natural look combined with avant-garde toilets and bidet.

Flooring and wall coverings

There are a host of alternatives to the customary ceramic tiles. Corrugated aluminum sheets, dovetailed wood, and decorative painting are just some of the options to be borne in mind.

Wooden flooring and walls lined with corrugated aluminum sheets in this house built by John Mainwaring in Queensland, Australia.

Bathtub covered with ceramics, using the *trencadis* technique.

Masonry walls and a shower lined with pinewood for a rustic bathroom in a house in the mountains.

Lacquered dovetailed wood is used to define a perimeter panel covering half the wall height.

Very dark tropical wood and a marble top surrounding porcelain sinks.

Here tiles are used to cover both the floor and the walls.

Sinks made to measure

Despite the vast range of sinks, pedestals, and faucets on the market, there are still some people who prefer a piece made to measure. This personal commission may only affect the support or bowl of the sink, or it may cover the faucets and piping. However, in all these cases the decision to participate in its design indicates a desire to confer a personal seal on the sink.

This sink belongs to a house built in 1994 in Capistrano Beach, CA, by Rob Wellington Quigley. The type of materials used and its distance from the other toilet fittings make this unusual sink resemble a baptismal font.

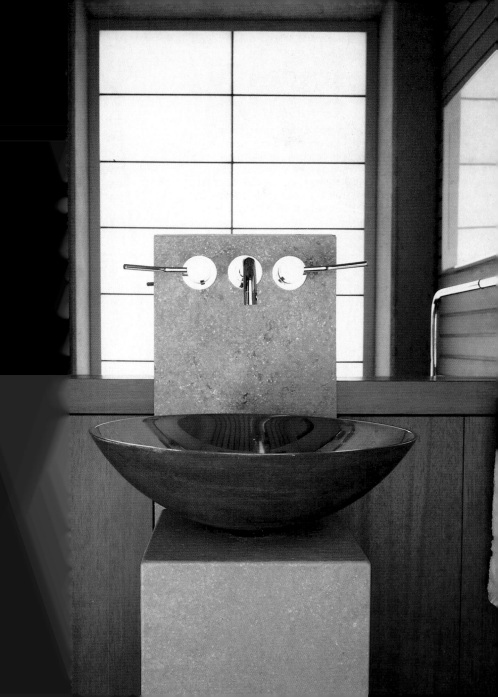

Peter Romaniuk has opted to put all the bathroom elements in the corridor leading to the bedrooms. It is therefore a passageway and not a private room. However, to achieve a certain degree of privacy this London architect has hung circular curtains round the various elements: sink, dressing table, and bathtub. Each of these circular spaces is illuminated by a skylight. The bathroom fittings are freestanding pieces reminiscent of the machines of the Swiss sculptor Jean Tinguely.

The privilege of space

Although it is a privilege that is difficult to enjoy, due to the lack of living space in the large cities, there are cases in which it is possible to indulge in large bathrooms, like those presented in these pages.

Residence on Lake Weyba in Australia. This is a water area designed by Gabriel Poole in 1996.

Complete bathroom of a house in Hanover, Germany. Design by Storch and Ehlers.

Porcelain

Porcelain is certainly the material that is most widely used in the construction of bathroom fittings, and this has often led it to be associated with characterless and unsophisticated bathrooms. However, porcelain is a material with huge possibilities, not only because it stands up so well to water and is easy to manufacture, but also because of the wealth of images it can conjure up as a result of its long history in the world of bathrooms.

Porcelain sink from Boffi.

Faucet from the *Tara* series for fitting into walls, designed by Dieter Sieger for Dornbracht.

Porcelain sink designed by Philippe Starck for Duravit.

Charles sink, designed by Giampaolo Benedini for Agape.

Glass surfaces

Rapsel has gone further than most, and its catalog features sinks with transparent bowls. *Homage to Sheila* by Gianluigi Landoni.

Coup de foudre by Shiro Kuramata.

Glass is becoming more and more popular in bathrooms. Its transparency is attractive in a space where clean and shiny surfaces are essential.

Stainless steel

Although stainless steel is usually only used for the faucets and the bowl of the sink, the use of this material has spread to the point where some pieces are made entirely out of stainless steel.

Wing, designed by Gianluigi Landoni for Rapsel.

Euclide sink tower, designed in 1984 by Finn Skodt and distributed by Rapsel.

Optimo sink from Sloan. Industrial designs have been gradually incorporated into the domestic environment.

Morgans sink designed by Andrée Putman. It includes a series of accessories.

Menhir, a model by Giampaolo Benedini for Agape.

Fino (1990),
for Solo Möbel.

Herbert Ludwikowski

The simplicity of form in Ludwikowski's pieces enables his objects to fit into all types of settings. In fact, his main aim is precisely to endow his pieces with enough independence for them to function as autonomous objects.

Swing (1992),
for Solo Möbel

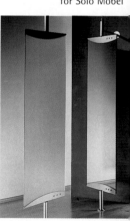

Laser mirror furnishing (1989), for Solo Möbel. The sink is designed by Berger & Stahl for Rapsel.

Calypso (1994),
for Solo Möbel

America's Cup (1993),
for Rapsel.

Sink with a pedestal

Positano, designed by Matteo Thun in 1997 for Rapsel. Enameled ceramic sink in terracotta or white. The cupboards featured on either side are by Gunilla Allard.

Bagnella, designed by Dieter Sieger for Duravit. This is a collection that includes various models, with slight formal modifications and changes in material. There is also a series of complementary accessories to match.

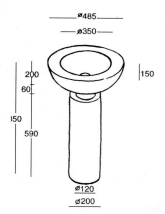

Ø485
Ø350
200
60
150
)50
590
Ø120
Ø200

Showers

New Haven
shower base.
Villeroy & Boch.

Isly. Jacob
Delafon.

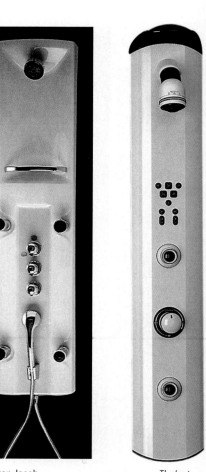

Iristor. Jacob
Delafon.

Tholastar.
Jacob Delafon.

Kattara base.
Jacob Delafon.

Djerbo base.
Jacob Delafon

Punch base.
Jacob Delafon.

Tonus base.
Jacob Delafon.

Trocadero
shower base.
Jacob Delafon.

Báltica base.
Jacob Delafon.

Closets

Viala. Creative System.

Universo high closet.

Universo makeup closet.

High closet. Villeroy & Boch.

Swivel Cabinet. Lavillette.

New Haven. Villeroy & Boch.

New Haven. Villeroy & Boch.

High closet. Villeroy & Boch.

Symphonie. Giomo.

Bidets

Trocadero.
Jacob Delafon.

New Haven.
Villeroy & Boch.

Astros.
Jacob Delafon.

Portrait.
Jacob Delafon.

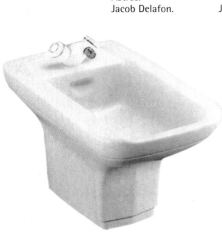

Fleur.
Jacob Delafon.

Antores.
Jacob Delafeon.

Altair.
Jacob Delafon.

Veranda. Roca.

Odeon.
Jacob Delafon.

Sinks

Duo. Jacob Delafon.

Altair. Jacob Delafon.

Obina.
Dorn Bracht.

Aldo. Bagnella.

Vito. Bagnella.

Giula. Bagnella.

Laura. Bagnella.

Epura Modern Home. Villeroy & Boch.

Sink by Lavillette.

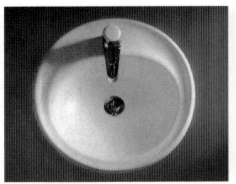

Manva sink.

Bali sink.

Duraplus sink.

Morea sink.

Caro sink.

Darling sink.

Dellorco sink.

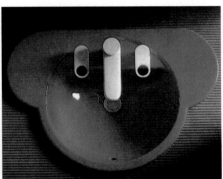

Orchidee sink.

Laconda sink.

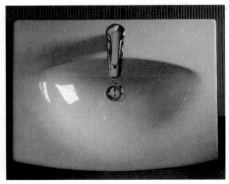

Giamo sink.

Dellarco sink.

Caro sink.

Darling sink.

Epura Cottage.
Villeroy & Boch.

Astros. Jacob Delafon.

Revival.
Jacob Delafon.

Fleur. Jacob Delafon.

Portrait. Jacob Delafon.

Trocadero.
Jacob Delafon.

New Haven.
Villeroy & Boch.

New Haven.
Villeroy & Boch.

Bathtubs

New Haven. Villeroy & Boch.

Portrait cast-iron bathtub. Jacob Delafon.

Revival cast-iron bathtub. Jacob Delafon.

Fleur cast-iron bathtub. Jacob Delafon.

Ceta.

Vahina methacrylate bathtub. Jacob Delafon.

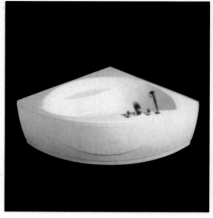

Laelia methacrylate bathtub. Jacob Delafon.

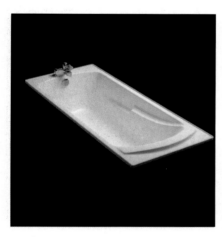

Amalia methacrylate bathtub. Jacob Delafon.

Odyssea methacrylate bathtub. Jacob Delafon.

Astros cast-iron bathtub. Jacob Delafon.

Odeon methacrylate bathtub. Jacob Delafon.

Altair cast-iron bathtub. Jacob Delafon.

Trocadero cast-iron bathtub. Jacob Delafon.

Antores cast-iron bathtub. Jacob Delafon.

Super Repos hydromassage tub. Jacob Delafon.

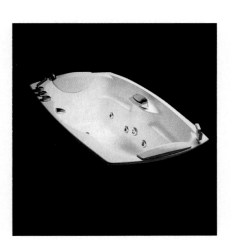

Trocadero hydromassage tub. Jacob Delafon.

Astros hydromassage tub. Jacob Delafon.

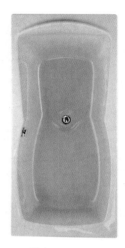

Viala.

Magnum.

Gran Gracia.

Helios.

Libra.

Taurus.

Opera.

Cetus.

Stratos.

Zenith.

Amadea.

Tiora.

Tucana

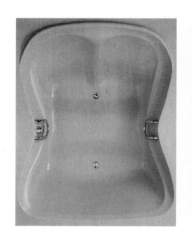

Antibes.

Benodet.

Deauville.

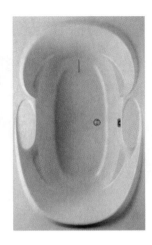

Belle Ille.

Oleron.

Honfleur.

Menton.

Sagitta.

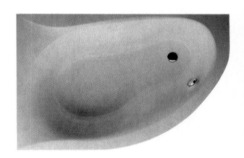

Porquerolles.

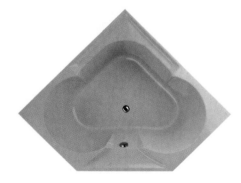

Camaret.

Croisic.

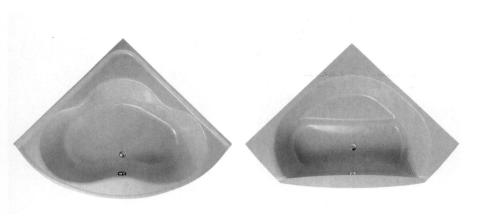

Royan.

La Naupole.

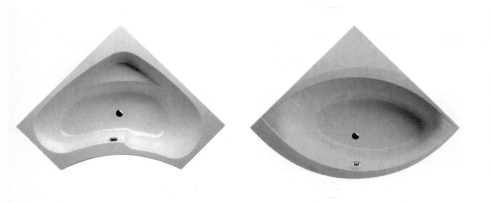

Quiberon.

Pallas.

Toilets

Postrait. Jacob Delafon.

Odeon. Jacob Delafon.

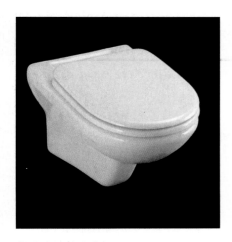

Altair. Jacob Delafon.

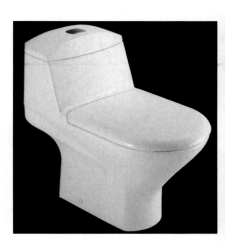

Trocadero. Jacob Delafon.

Antores. Jacob Delafon.

Atila. Jacob Delafon.

Fleur. Jacob Delafon.

Astros. Jacob Delafon.

Revival. Jacob Delafon.

Maternelle. Jacob Delafon.

Raised toilet. Jacob Delafon.

Raised independent toilet. Jacob Delafon.

Helios. Villeroy & Boch.

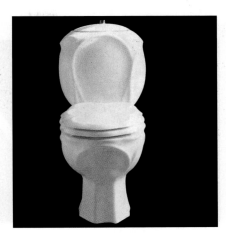

Orchidee. Jacob Delafon.

Veranda. Roca.

New Haven. Villeroy & Boch.

Faucets

Single control for
Trocadero sink.
Jacob Delafon.

Topkapi faucet.
Jacob Delafon.

Single control
Palacio faucet.
Jacob Delafon.

Tao single
control faucet.
Jacob Delafon.

Single control
for *Cip* sink.
Jacob Delafon.

Monoblock from
the *Galatea* bidet.
Jacob Delafon.

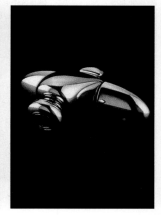

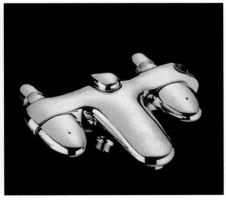

Monoblock from the
Galatea sink.
Jacob Delafon.

Topkapi faucet
with *Fleur* handles.
Jacob Delafon.

Mixer for shower.
Jacob Delafon.

Wall mixer for
bath and shower.
Jacob Delafon.

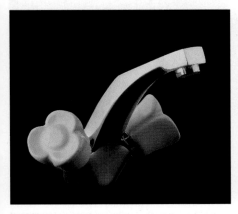

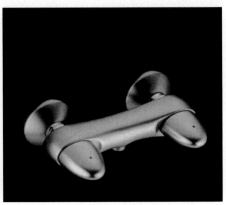

Ensemble for bath and
shower. Jacob Delafon.

Wall mixer for the *Topkapi*
shower. Jacob Delafon.

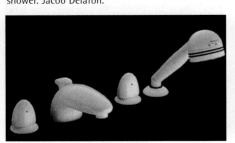

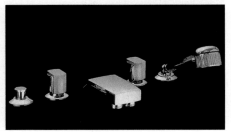

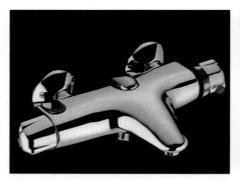

Thermostat for *Ultima* bath and shower. Jacob Delafon.

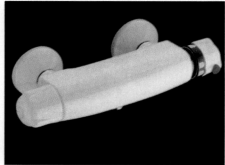

Thermostat for *Ultima* shower. Jacob Delafon.

Ensemble for *Trocadero* bath and shower. Jacob Delafon.

Ensemble for *Palacio* sink and bidet with low spout. Jacob Delafon.

Ensemble for *Palacio* bath and shower. Jacob Delafon.

Ensemble for *Palacio* bath and shower. Jacob Delafon.

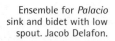

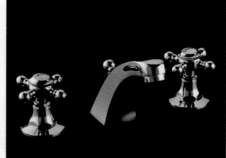

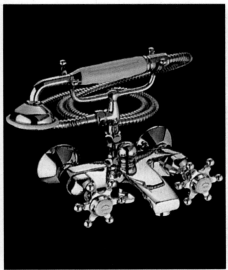

Wall mixer for
Palacio bath and
shower. Jacob
Delafon.

Ensemble for *Postrait*
bath and shower.
Jacob Delafon.

Wall mixer for *Postrait*
bath and shower.
Jacob Delafon.

Wall mixer for
Postrait shower.
Jacob Delafon.

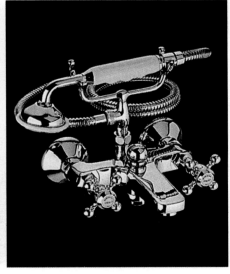

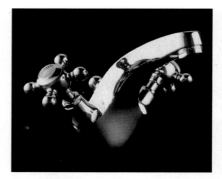

Monoblock for
Postrait sink and
bidet. Jacob Delafon.

Single wall control for
Elosis bath and shower.
Jacob Delafon.

Ensemble for
Palacio sink with
high spout.
Jacob Delafon.

Single control for
the *Elosis* sink.
Jacob Delafon.

Ensemble for
Galatea sink.
Jacob Delafon.

Single control for
Elosis bath and
shower.
Jacob Delafon.

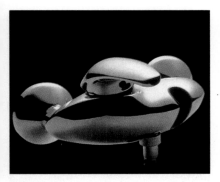

Single wall control
for *Elosis* shower.
Jacob Delafon.

Ensemble for *O* sink.
Jacob Delafon.

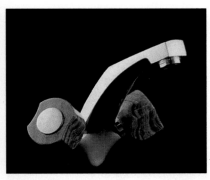

Monoblock for
Topkapi sink.
Jacob Delafon.

Monoblock for
Topkapi bidet.
Jacob Delafon.

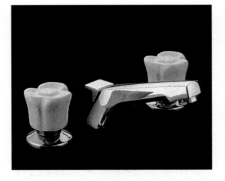

Wall mixer for
Topkapi bath and
shower. Jacob Delafon.

Ensemble for *Topkapi*
sink and bidet.
Jacob Delafon.

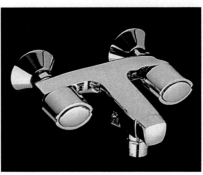

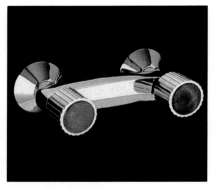

Wall mixer for *Topkapi* shower. Jacob Delafon.

Pulsomat Surf. Grohe

Pulsoactron. Grohe   *Pulsoactron* wall faucet. Grohe.

Contropress faucet. Grohe   In-built *Pulsoactron* faucet. Grohe.

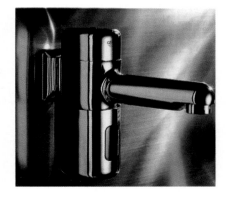

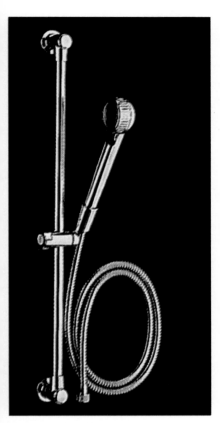

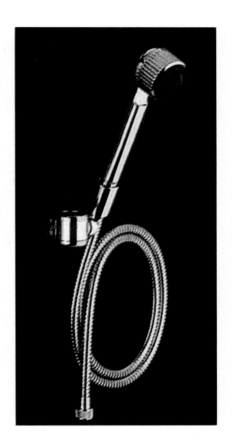

Four wall mixers for
Topkapi bath and shower.
Jacob Delafon.

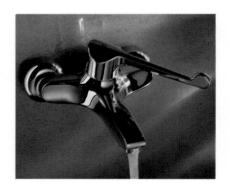

Euroeco faucet. Grohe.

Taron faucet. Grohe.

Ensemble for *Sinfonia* sink. Grohe.

Chiara faucet. Grohe.

Eurotrend faucet. Grohe.

Sentosa faucet. Grohe.

Grohtherm 3000
mixer. Grohe.

Europlus faucet. Grohe.

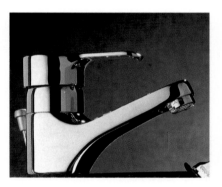

Eurowing faucet. Grohe.

Eurodisc faucet. Grohe.

Eurodur faucet. Grohe.

Atlanta faucet. Grohe.

Zedra. Grohe

Supra. Grohe

Relexa Plus
shower. Grohe.

Adria Hit. Grohe

Automatic 2000. Grohe

Polaris

Madison

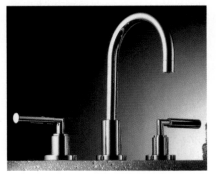

Point. Sieger Design

Fino. Sieger Design

Tara Classic.
Sieger Design

Tara. Sieger Design

Tara ensemble.
Sieger Design.

Tara mixer.
Sieger Design.

Meta Pur.
Sieger Design

Meta Luce Colour.
Sieger Design

Meta Classic.
Sieger Design

Meta Nova.
Sieger Design

New Haven. Grohe

Terraces

The terrace represents a privilege, especially for people who live in city centers overrun by asphalt. This exterior space affords contact with nature in the privacy of the home. It is possible to endow it with both visual appeal and a functional purpose if we choose the appropriate furniture and accessories. How we furnish the terrace must depend on its size and position, and the activities we wish to pursue there.

If space and budget permit we can opt to put a swimming pool in the terrace, although this is a decision that must be pondered thoroughly because a pool requires a certain amount of maintenance and therefore expense. It can greatly embellish our yard or terrace because it creates a striking focus of both color and light. The swimming pool, which must be put in an area that catches the sun without being exposed to too much wind, can assume various shapes: rectangular, circular, L shape or anything else that takes our fancy. It is absolutely essential that the walls of the pool are covered effectively: mosaic and PVC resist water well, whilst other options include glass, resin tiles, or special pool paint — which is the cheapest alternative.

In the heat of the summer, our body either urges us to take advantage of the sun and get a tan in a comfortable beach chair or begs for shelter from the broiling sun in the shade of a porch, an awning, a pergola, or a summerhouse. It is more than likely that, time and weather permitting, we shall pass long spells on the terrace. This means that we must take great pains over our choice of furniture because, being at the mercy of the weather, it will receive some rough treatment. It is obvious, then, that one of the determining factors in our choice of materials must be their assured durability.

The furniture most often found on a terrace comprises chairs, beach chairs, armchairs, and tables, and these come in a wide array of designs and colors. Ideally we should consider furniture that does not involve an

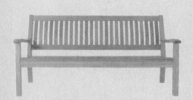

abrupt break with the style of the home itself, especially if the terrace is an extension of the dining room or the living room. There is a very wide range of materials to choose from. We can plump for metals like aluminum and iron, that are not altered by the sun, or woods like teak, beech, pine, and ash, although the last three are somewhat delicate. Resin is another option; it is very resistant and can be cleaned with soap and water. If we want chairs made of fabric, we must bear in mind that canvas refracts the heat, and that cotton and polyester are more benevolent. Many people prefer vegetable fibers like wicker and cane that can be easily cleaned, although they are more delicate.

Most terraces are an extension of the interior of the home, and only a few have the benefit of being surrounded by a yard. This distinction is important because each requires a different decorative approach. In the first type, we want to create a relaxing environment, more carefree than the home itself, and so we can decorate it with furniture and plants. The second type, on the other hand, does not require plants as it is already endowed with greenery. In either case, it is best to decorate the terrace with furniture that goes well with that of the lounge. If the house is in a rustic style, for example, terrace furniture in teak or vegetable fiber would be perfect. The space on the terrace can be divided up in various ways. One very common and practical solution is the creation of two distinct environments, one for eating and the other for relaxing and conversing.

There is nothing quite as enjoyable as having summer meals and get-togethers with family and friends in an inviting nook. If our terrace looks out on the street and we want to protect our privacy from neighbors and passersby, the best solution is plants and awnings. Another very cozy option that provides a wonderful finishing touch to a house is a porch that protects us from the vagaries of the weather and offers us an oasis of peace and security.

A classic-style architectural element enclosing one corner of the swimming pool bestows on the setting the romantic personality of a Renaissance villa.

Building around water

A swimming pool is not only a highly prized addition to a family home, it also gives rise to original ways of making it fit into a yard. The strong contrast between water and solid building materials opens up a wide range of solutions, from the daring and dynamic to the more traditional.

The presence of a lawn, with the blue of the pool breaking the monotony of the green, offers a simple way of providing relaxation.

This swimming pool is distinguished by the interplay of its geometrical forms and the materials with which it is constructed. The irregular shape bordering the grass contrasts with the linearity and sobriety of the wood.

The architecture of this cabin, made entirely of wood, is coordinated with the decking running alongside the swimming pool, and sets off the striking detail furnished by the white canvas.

T-shaped swimming pool, topped off by a porch opening out onto the water. The design by Wolf Siegfried Wagner takes advantage of an ancient Hispano-Arab irrigation canal.

Swimming pool built by Giovanni Melillo inside an old villa.
The masonry walls and the lawn immediately surrounding the
water enable the setting to blend in unobtrusively with the
classic architecture.

The absence of any protective structure does not deprive this space of the feel of a covered terrace. Slightly raised, enclosed with greenery and topped off with an awning, this terrace creates a transition area between the house and the yard.

Porches

The porch, built slightly above ground level, is conceived as a quiet relaxed spot ideal for informal meetings and chats. The horizontal covering, that not only totally covers the terrace area but also protects the entrance to the home itself, can be made of a variety of materials and supported by pillars that dominate the space and give it its special character.

A spectacular porch beside a swimming pool designed by Alberto Aguirre. The proximity of the water means that its relaxing effects can be enjoyed in a very lively space.

A classic structure for an austere porch that serves as a dining room – almost in the open air.

The large extension
of the lawn gives this
porch the air of a
gallery for relaxed
conversations.

Classic porch with a white balustrade running
parallel to the house. This type of space is closer to
the house than the yard, but the furniture is
arranged to face the yard.

Porch-terrace with colonial style
decoration. The lack of any architectural
features to mark the boundaries of this
space is overcome by the addition of a
structure made from metal and canvas.

Partially covered terraces

These terraces, built with a whole host of materials, benefit from the introduction of greenery. Nowadays the effects of intermittent shadow can be achieved with adjustable roofs in sophisticated materials that effectively resist the inclemency of the weather.

A covering made of natural fibers, placed in front of the porch, creates a transitional space between the building and the open air.

The finishings of this classic white pergola with details like the decorated capitals of the pillars hint at a Greco-Roman style.

This covering made of wooden planks in the manner of a pergola gives this terrace a style of its own. Underneath, the setting takes on an exotic air, thanks to the semitropical vegetation and the vivid colors of the rugs and upholstery.

The vivid reds and yellows give an exotic look to this setting, which is intensified by the intense green of the vegetation.

A structure made of untreated natural wood. The regular distribution of the logs on the covering softens the impact of the sun on the couch and table.

A covering made of canes and branches roughly bound together. These types of structures permit a quick change to the amount of sun coming in, and create an attractive space with a simple traditional character.

Teklassic is responsible for this design in functional straight lines, distinguished by the quality and durability of the wood.

Tables for the terrace

The table is a meeting point and maybe the main focus of the conversation area. Outdoor tables are the most practical and versatile element of a terrace, as they can serve as dining tables, containers, and center tables all at the same time.

Ensemble in metal by Teklassic with a table topped with mosaic. The different combinations of the mosaic increase a table's decorative possibilities and make it the central feature of the setting.

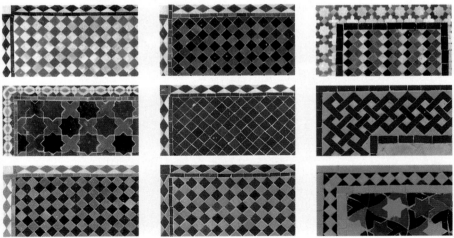

This glass and metal table from the *Victoria* collection by Hugonet presents a solid rational design, capable of resisting any climate without losing its discreet elegance.

Another glass and metal table from the *Victoria* series by Hugonet. Its oval shape means that it can seat more guests as it eliminates any dead corners.

Cornwall rectangular table from Garpa. The versatility of this rectangular design is enhanced by the extension module enclosed within the table itself. Below, a view of the extension system.

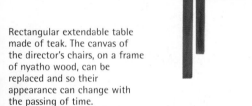

Rectangular extendable table made of teak. The canvas of the director's chairs, on a frame of nyatho wood, can be replaced and so their appearance can change with the passing of time.

Serving trolley from Habitat that makes it possible to take all the food required for meals onto the terrace.

Backup furniture

The terrace, often the only outdoor part of a home and moreover with restrictions on space, must nevertheless adapt to several different requirements over the course of a day. This has led to the emergence of a wide range of backup furniture and seats that are light and easy to store and arrange on the space.

Teklassic table made of dark teak.

Reims bottle cooler. Made of teak and lined with polypropylene, it has a capacity of twelve bottles.

Folding teak tables from Habitat. They hardly occupy any space and are easy to move around to suit the task.

The *Richmond* trolley from Teklassic has several drawers and accessories that make it extremely practical.

Outdoor seats

Yards and terraces have become an integral part of the home itself, forming a unit subject to the same criteria for their decoration. As a result, outdoor pieces of furniture are increasingly being considered as visually attractive in their own right, and nowadays models are on offer to match the most diverse kinds of yard.

Bench from the *Atlante* series by Hugonet. Comfort and visual appeal with a minimalist touch.

The *Sissinghurst* model from the Teklassic company, a replica of the original still in the gardens of Sissinghurst Castle in England, owned by the National Trust.

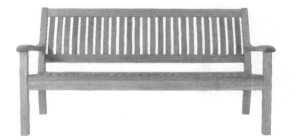

Left and above: The *Manor* seats and benches seek the maximum of comfort by incorporating contours into the backs and seats to combine functionality with elegance.

The circular *Glenham* bench, with a hexagonal center, is made by Teklassic. Its austere lines and natural wood finish allow it to blend into the landscape, and give it a private and intimate character.

Detail of the circular *Glenham* bench.

View of the *Glenham* corner bench.

Teklassic's *Glenham* can also be made at right angles to create a corner that closes an area off from the vegetation.

Under the shadow of a parasol

This design with a square top is by Hugonet, and its finishing has striking details, like its all-white color and the sphere at the top of its axis, that give it a touch of elegance.

The parasol has a top that protects a space from changes in sunlight. To serve this practical purpose, it must combine resistance to climatic extremes with visual charm.

The flat top is the distinguishing feature of this parasol by Roland Vlaemynck, made with a dark wooden frame and colored fabric.

A terrace with a tropical atmosphere that has a parasol that seems to mimic the natural forms of the palm trees.

Under the shadow of a parasol

Parasol made of pale-colored wood and white fabric. The lack of tension between the spokes of the shade gives it a rough and original touch.

The parasol supported from the side has made great technical advances and is now a highly practical and attractive alternative for large areas.

Awning from the *Patio Bois* collection from Teklassic, in white on a wooden frame.

Straight lines for a terrace situated next to a swimming pool. The luminosity of the white canvas contrasts with the colors of the vegetation.

Rustic atmosphere for a swimming pool terrace. The parasol creates an intimate setting for the furniture.

The blue canvas of these parasols seeks to match the color of the swimming pool.

Reclining loungers

Reclining chairs and loungers, the most luxurious elements in a terrace or yard, are manufactured according to rigorous criteria of comfort and esthetics.

View of the teak structure of the *Commodore* model from Teklassic.

Reclining chair made of aluminum and fabric, with teak armrests. The *Sunset* model incorporates a reclining mechanism with a footrest that allows it to turn into a lounger.

Reclining *Commodore* chair with footrest. Classic lounger with polished bronze fittings.

The dramatic impact of white fabric in terraces and yards has a practical aspect, as white reflects the sun and is easy to coordinate with other furnishings and accessories.

Habitat presents models with a simple comfortable structure that combine a practical design with some original details.

Lounger from the *Atlante* series by Hugonet, made of metal and fabric.

A surprising structure made in teak by Habitat. The design suggests both practicality and durability.

Teak, stainless steel, and canvas are the three materials that make up this very simple *Riviera* lounger.

El Patio de Marta is responsible for the simple and functional forms of this beach chair. Its various positions and portability, together with the combination of white with wood make it ideal for any setting.

Lounger made in teak by the Van Notten company. The wooden structure with vertical bars is a classic in terraces and yards.

Natural fibers

The design of outdoor furniture made of natural fibers like cane and wicker adds details that evoke their natural origins and imbue them with a studied lack of sophistication. When they have been suitably treated, these fibers can be used to model backs and seats in rounded ergonomic forms that prove extremely comfortable.

This seat from the Habitat collection is made of cane. The simple way in which the fiber is modeled allows it to form one single element.

The *Loom* series by Teklassic creates very simple forms that are very comfortable. The lightness of these pieces, allowing them to be moved around without hesitation, increases their versatility.

Jubilee

Contract

Diamante

Mission. Very comfortable and simply designed
models manufactured by Teklassic.

The wealth of details created by the
intermeshed fibers permit combinations
with a variety of styles and materials.

The shape of the couch recalls the
classic *Chester* design.

Metal on the terrace

Technological advances have resulted in a notable evolution of outdoor metal furniture. The incorporation of new alloys has been accompanied by new treatments that lengthen the life of traditional methods. There has also been a trend toward thinner lines, and even wrought iron has shed its rustic image to embrace lighter and more refined forms. Outdoor furniture made of metal is as strong as ever, but these days it also combines practicality and elegant design.

Bright colors for the *New York* stacking chair from Hugonet. It is made of metal and canvas.

Croisette chair from Teklassic. There is a self-evident classic inspiration in this wrought-iron model that sets off the dark tones of the metal against the white of the cushion.

Croisette chair in a combination using a mat saffron color.

San Diego collection from Teklassic. The design and finish of this company won it an Oscar for the best collection in wrought iron at the International Salon in Chicago.

View of *San Diego* chairs from Teklassic. The top version features elegant armrests.

Palma chaise longue from Teklassic.

The strong lines, the combination of gray and mat black, and the arrangement of the furniture recreates the atmosphere of an elegant living room in the open air with this design by Hugonet.

Chair from the *Atlante* collection from Hugonet. The combination of blue and white and its sharply defined shape give it its own individual character.

Malibu chair from Hugonet. Functionality and absolute simplicity in a design with an original look.

Sobriety and elegance in a suite for the yard in dark green and white.

Combining metal and wood

The combination of metal and wood brings together strength and warmth. The strength lies in the metal structure that guarantees durability, whilst the finishing in wood provides comfort and visual charm. Direct contact with wood is more agreeable than with metal, and also allows us to dispense with cushions and textiles and enjoy the resulting interplay of tones and textures.

Center table from Hugonet lacquered in white, with a perforated wooden top.

View of chair with armrests from the *Fontenay* collection by Garpa.

The comfortable classic forms of the *Fontenay* ensemble from the Garpa company combine mat black and natural wood.

Atlante collection from Hugonet. Simplicity of forms in an ensemble that combines lacquered metal with wooden details for added elegance.

Monterrey is a collection from Teklassic in aluminum and teak. The wood in the back, seat, and armrests provides comfort.

Absolute simplicity in folding chairs made of metal and wood. These are a good solution for terraces with limited seating areas or storage space.

Wood

Wood is one of the most traditional materials used for making outdoor furniture, and its great durability and flexibility leads to designs of high quality and a strong visual impact. Current trends in furniture pursue the colonial tradition by incorporating exotic woods that are extremely resistant and require minimal upkeep. The characteristics of these materials have given rise to designs with a classic touch that seek a look that will not become dated, as this furniture is built to last for many years.

Babaco is a hammock from Habitat, made of solid nyatoh treated with oil. The arrangement of the wooden strips, attached to nylon runners, is both functional and attractive.

Tecdeco set from Roland Vlaemynck. The wood has been treated in a rougher manner to convey the impression of solidity.

Iruba collection from Grosfilex. It is practical and functional, with its pale-colored wood finish providing a total image of warm elegance.

Walden ensemble from the Lister company. The classic design of the table and chairs ensures that its look will transcend any passing fashions and not become dated during the long life of this teak furniture.

Esterel is a combination of teak and white canvas by Roland Vlaemynck. The setting has strong horizontal planes, thanks to the arrangement of the chairs, the table, and the wide parasol.

A combination of austere lines and generous solidity. The dark colors and the sobriety of the design give it a special elegance.

Today's designs make it possible to put outdoor furniture in interior settings giving onto the terrace.

Trolley from Habitat. It is made entirely of wood, even the wheels, which demonstrate a very dynamic and versatile design.

A close-up of the *Esterel* chair by Roland Vlaemynck.

Views of the *Kent* chair, with and without armrests, from Teklassic.

The *Ashburnham* bench is designed by the English company Lister. The structure, with its strong upward thrust and great solidity, endows it with an extremely distinctive personality that enables it to reign in isolation over any part of the yard.

Plastic materials

Ensembles made in resins and plastics for outdoor use offer a wide variety of design possibilities, thanks to their malleability. Colors and forms both seek to combine visual appeal with comfort, whilst also offering easy maintenance and great resistance to inclement weather.

Fidji Evolution lounger in Baltic blue from Grosfillex. Not only is it extremely comfortable, but it also has a practical drawer hidden behind the backrest.

Roland Vlaemynck presents the *Rovergarden* furniture, comprising the *Toce Clásica* table and the *Cellina* folding chair. Both pieces are made of solid synthetic resin.

Ensemble from Grosfillex in a resin stained green. The main characteristic of pieces of outdoor furniture made out of resin is the great comfort they offer on account of their multiposition systems.

Grosfillex is responsible for the *Classic Fidji* ensemble. A painstaking design that offers great comfort through the dual position system incorporated into the seats.

Master lounger from Jardiland. Classic design for a comfortable complement to the swimming pool design.

Acadia armchair from Grosfillex with a back that can be adjusted in four positions. The ensemble is completed by the *Vega* table in green and granite.

Canvas

The use of canvas and padding in outdoor furniture combines functionality, esthetics, and good value, making these materials suitable for any kind of terrace.
Canvas makes it possible to use vivid colors that break up the monotony of wood and achieve a versatile and casual look, as most chairs made with this material are folding.

Jardiland offers an ensemble made of wood and green canvas. The upholstery of the chairs can be coordinated with other accessories, such as colorful rugs and tablecloths.

The *Bass* chair is a model from Jardiland made out of dark red maranti wood and acrylic canvas. The seat is reinforced with strong elastic mesh to give it greater stability and comfort.

Roland Vlaemynck offers an ensemble of linear simplicity and comfort made of teak and padded acrylic canvas.

Close-up of the folding
chair by Roland
Vlaemynck, made in
white acrylic canvas.

Folding chair made in teak and
padded acrylic canvas. Acrylic canvas
guarantees a degree of permanency
in the dyeing that will not
deteriorate in sunlight.

A beach chair with arms and an added wooden footrest for greater comfort.

Safari chair from Teklassic made of wood and canvas. The collection, made in natural colors, aims to match the shades already found in an outside setting.

Colorful terraces

Painted woods, structures finished with canvas, awnings, flowerpots: outdoor accessories in intense vivid colors lend a very carefree and relaxing tone that strengthens a terrace's credentials as a space for leisure activities. The diversity of materials used in outdoor furniture and fittings offers finishings able to resist sunlight and the inclemency of the weather.

An original table made from a huge spool intended for industrial cable is surrounded by brightly colored chairs to present a highly amusing and fun-loving image.

Loom chair made in natural fibers dyed green. The Kettal company updates a classic of terrace furniture.

Deco ensemble made of smelted aluminum that has been painted red. This design from the Kettal company is inspired by Modernist architects like Gaudí.

Ensemble made out of resin by the Kettal company. The shades of bamboo and coconut blend perfectly to provide a very elegant finish.

Terrace ensemble with an awning designed by Roland Vlaemynck in blue with touches of green. These two colors are very suitable in terraces next to a swimming pool, since they echo the colors of the water.

Well balanced proportions for a terrace that seeks to emphasize the natural tones of all its various components.

Smelted and painted aluminum is the basis for the *Mitos* chair from Kettal. The obvious classic inspiration for this collection is further heightened by the cushion upholstered with a design of plant motifs.

The *Mekony* earthenware jar, the *Oval* flowerpots and fruit bowl, and the *Nemo* pitcher, all from Habitat, are accessories that bestow splashes of color on a terrace.

Ensemble in wood and orange-colored fabrics that complement the flower arrangements.

Brightly colored combination in a rustic-style terrace. The intensity of the shades of red contrasts with the green of the decoration.

Details of the flower arrangement in the photo below, coordinated with a tablecloth for outdoor use from Jardiland.

Ensemble made of teak and yellow-colored fabrics. The flower arrangement matches both the upholstery and the flowerpots.

Brilliant white

White has classic status for terraces, as it reflects light and presents a clean yet informal look. White's versatility lies in the fact that it can be combined with any other color that might be found outdoors. It is also easy to clean and does not fade with sunlight.

The parasol in white acrylic canvas defines a space in this suite by Roland Vlaemynck.

Flowerpot holder in wood that has been lacquered in white to brighten it up.

Terrace running horizontally in front of a building. The white of the walls and floors gives it a very dynamic finish.

Classic Menorca model from Kettal.
Made of natural fiber and
upholstered in blue and white. A
romantic look for a suite with clear
references to tradition.

Ensemble formed entirely by all-white
components. Resins, fabrics, and lacquered
metals provide a monochrome finish boasting
luminosity and freshness. Composition by
Roland Vlaemynck.

Mondrian chair made in African teak by Kettal. The combination of pale wood with white produces a very elegant and uncluttered effect.

Comfortable ensemble in wicker, with white upholstery. The play of light and the treatments applied to each material give rise to tonal nuances with a great visual impact.

In blue

Blue is one of the classic colors of exterior decoration, along with white and the various shades of wood. Canvas, plastic material, and even stained wood use blue to create a rapport with the sea or swimming pool. The range of intense but elegant blues currently on the market aims to endow yards and terraces with a distinctive Mediterranean look.

The blue area echoes the swimming pool that dominates this exterior.

Ensemble made up of nyatoh and blue canvas. The three classic outdoor colors in a perfect mix.

Shades of blue for a terrace with a marked Mediterranean character. The brilliance of the white is a perfect match for the elegance of the blue.

Vegetation in the starring role

When we lay out a yard or terrace the vegetation becomes an architectural element in its own right that suggests which spaces should be filled with furniture. Yard design offers a huge range of options, drawing on color, form, and texture, but it is also subject to a host of conditioning factors, which mean that the end result is always unique and unrepeatable. We can use greenery to create areas for eating, strolling, or even swimming.

The unruliness in the background of this yard contrasts with the precise vertical lines of the two trees that flank the entrance to this space.

Metal bench made by Sia El Mercado de Flores. The design of many pieces of outdoor furniture is based on the vegetation that surrounds them.

Balmoral ensemble from Teklassic. The discreet transparency of the chairs allows the outdoor vegetation to take pride of place.

Front view of a pergola made of metal and wood. The simplicity of the upper section evokes the delicacy that the branches of a tree make against the sky.

Bamboo is the material that marks out this space dominated by tonal contrasts.

A composition made up of natural landmarks can contain dozens of details or a single element that captures the onlooker's attention. Here a large tree and a pond vie for superiority in this peaceful rural landscape.

Flowers have started to invade the walls of this outhouse. The interaction between architecture and vegetation seems to assert the importance of the latter as one of the main sources of inspiration for architects and designers.

Outdoor chairs made of metal. The complex lines of their metallic tubular structure try to reflect the richness of the vegetation that dominates this yard.

Old gardening accessories can be turned into striking decorative elements. This romantic wheelbarrow sets off the faded colors of the aging wood with a colorful floral arrangement.

Decorative accessories

The presence of floral adornments as decorative elements in terraces and yards creates the need for complementary accessories that require both functionality and visual appeal. The latter is especially important, as they provide visual details that give an outdoor environment a more personal character.

Elongated conical vase made in wood by Jardiland.

Original flowerpot holders made of wicker with a metal support, from the Sia company.

Another view of the conical vases from Jardiland, this time in different sizes.

Green vase made by Jardiland. Its color contrasts with that of the teak surface of the table.

Jardilan presents this
collection of jars with
a metallic zinc finish.

Pottery
vase and
flowerpots
from Jardiland.

Folding
rectangular table
in teak, on which
some decorative
flowerpots have
been placed. The
dark bucket
contrasts with
the breezy colors
of the rest of the
setting.
Jardiland.

The octagonal table is decorated with a group of vases made of fiber and wood. Jardiland.

Elegant combination of colors in these flowerpots on stands from Sia.

A group of painted pottery flowerpots on a chest of drawers contrast with the metal elements and the white of the furniture.

Flowerpot with aged finish. Teklassic.

Lighting

It is advisable to plan the lighting at the same time as the rest of the decoration. In fact, it is best to do this right at the beginning, before we put in any furniture or start to decorate anything. This has the following advantages: it is easier to define each space within the room, the electrical installation can be planned down to the last detail, a harmonious visual effect is obtained with less effort, and we can even save money.

Normally, the lighting is left to the end of the decorative process, or is considered as a separate item. Whether or not it is planned from the beginning, lighting should not be a problem for us. If we follow some basic rules, it is easy to devise a lighting scheme that is sure to succeed.

Firstly, we should examine the floor plan. The architectural layout will give us an overall idea of how we are going to light each room, bearing in mind where we are going to put the furniture. We should also check the availability of natural light during the course of the day and then decide what kind of artificial lighting we require.

Light is the most versatile of all the elements used to decorate a setting. However, artificial light is not our only resource. Sunlight will also be useful if we learn how to control its effects. Ultimately, sunshine lights our home for the greater part of the day, imbuing its interiors with life and modifying its intensity according to the time of day or season of the year. We therefore have to find out the direction of the sunlight coming through our windows and doors and try to use it to our fullest advantage when we arrange the space in the interior.

Let us suppose we have made a correct assessment of the natural light in our home. We then have to decide what type of artificial lighting is required, taking into account that lighting also serves to create atmosphere. Intense light instills energy and tends to encourage work or energetic activity. Subdued lighting makes us feel relaxed, although if there is too much it can also send us to sleep. Excessively strong light makes us avert our eyes and makes us feel physically and emotionally uncomfortable. Sharp contrasts between light and shade can create a very distinctive atmosphere, although they can be tiring if they are overdone.

There are three main types of lighting we can draw on when looking for the most suitable combination: general lighting, to provide a more or less uniform light; local lighting, which is used for specific activities like reading or sewing; and decorative lighting that serves to pick out special areas or objects, and enhance color schemes.

All the lamps and accessories we need to achieve these different effects are at hand. Hanging lights provide good general lighting, but they tend to produce shadows and do not help tasks like reading and sewing. The amount of light shed depends on the type of shade used and the height at which it is hung. Table lights illuminate clearly defined areas that need to be well lit; according to the shade used, they can throw light upward, downward, or sideways. Standard lamps can supply either general or directional lighting, as some have spotlights that can be used to highlight specific objects or areas. Wall lamps are used to project light toward the ceiling or floor. Fluorescent lights require a special circuit that is large and difficult to hide, but they are long lasting and therefore cheaper than normal ones. Moreover, there are also very narrow miniature models available that are easy to conceal.

Spotlights give a good illustration of the dual role that can be played by lighting as, although they are essentially functional, they can also be used to create atmosphere. There are models made for normal light bulbs, others for large bulbs with a reflector incorporated, and yet others for halogen bulbs that project a very narrow beam. Adjustable spotlights occupy less space on the ceiling than in-built ones, and if they are used to light plants or corners from below they can produce some highly decorative effects.

Light in the living room

The lighting for the living room is one of the most important details in the home. It must be planned from several viewpoints to achieve a homogenous and relaxing setting. There are various alternatives that can exert an influence in this respect, by using colored light systems or shades that modify the light emanating from the lamp. The intensity must be suitable for a space intended for meetings and get-togethers. Today's lighting systems incorporate options that regulate their intensity and provide greater versatility. Another idea is to put several lamps in the living room that can pick out the specific areas being used, or the space can be endowed with more general illumination.

A large classic hanging lamp for a living room with a Mozarabic influence. Secondary wall lamps illuminate the ceiling and highlight the details of its elaborate decoration.

The furniture in this room has been placed against the walls to obtain a large central area. The large number of lamps heightens the luminosity and spaciousness of this 1930s-style room.

This bookcase, with an extending sidepiece, provides the basis of an original work table. The lamp is made along the same lines and suspended on a vertical axis from the top shelf.

A simple reading lamp lights up this couch made of natural fibers and wood. This space bears witness to a fascination for natural materials.

Living-dining room with two areas clearly marked by the large arch that dominates the setting. The lighting elements follow classic models to fit in with the generally rustic air.

The lighting style in this living-dining room reflects a decorative style with classic influences. The impression of comfort and warmth is heightened by the tone of the lighting, designed to evoke a feeling of snugness.

A large living room divided into three independent areas, each with its own function and, in consequence, different lighting requirements.

The lamps in this living room are made from different size pitchers that blend in with the classic atmosphere of the spacious setting.

Two table lamps are placed on either side of the alcove that dominates this space. The differences between the two lamps indicate a desire for an independent effect for each of the two areas.

The lighting in this living room is placed near the exterior in an attempt to define the interior space through the use of chiaroscuro.

An attic living room with classic influences. The lighting is supplied by two lamps reminiscent of old carbide lighting systems.

The pale colors in this living room suggest a desire to add to the luminosity of the space, confirmed by the incorporation of multiple light sources.

One corner of a living-dining room. The table lamp projects light in shades of ocher that is reflected on the wall to heighten the feeling of warmth. Three small lamps pick out the front of the old piece of office furniture, now turned into a bar.

Original standard lamp made of natural fibers. Its strange shape, like a giant glass, makes it the star of this room.

The two focal points of direct light are placed behind these interior loungers to produce a very dynamic effect.

Lighting for kitchens

The choice of a lighting system for kitchens is, along with that of the study area, one of the most complicated in the whole home. It must both provide general lighting and illuminate the work surfaces. Traditionally, the most commonly used systems have been fluorescent and neon lights that are long-lasting and do not use much electricity. These days the trend is to divide up the lighting and find the right solution for each individual space, according to criteria of functionality. Halogens for the work areas and lamps with an industrial design for general lighting provide attractive and versatile substitutes for the old tubes of cold light of earlier days.

Lighting is fundamental in a kitchen. Note how this combination of spotlights set into the ceiling does not allow any corner to be badly lit.

Lighting system giving an image based on the technical composition of its structure, in line with the setting's decorative style.

The lighting in this kitchen is sharply focused, with an emphasis on the work area and the table. However, the sunlight coming in through the window fills the space and means that artificial lighting is only required at night. *Polo* collection from Alta.

Front view of a small kitchen in which very bright materials have been used to convey the impression of greater space. The extractor hood has a lamp of its own to satisfy the lighting requirements for the cook while working at the hob.

The lamp suspended from the ceiling with all the kitchen elements in view enhances the appearance of an attractive, comfortable and practical kitchen.

A distinctive style for a kitchen in which the incorporation of modern halogens contrasts with the rustic details.

The placement of separate light sources for different work areas produces a powerful visual effect, thanks to the use of chiaroscuro. A light hanging from the ceiling lights the table. The illumination is completed by a decorative table lamp on the closet and another lamp above the cooking area, complemented by a powerful spotlight that provides all the light required for working.

Lamps with industrial design features that reproduce, in aluminum or stainless steel, the lighting systems formerly employed in factories and workshops make it possible to incorporate several identical elements without any need for complex installations.

The lighting in this kitchen, in an apartment in Barcelona's *Villa Olímpica* designed by Josep Juvé, is dominated by a line of bulbs of varying shapes and colors that provide original general lighting.

Decoration in a rustic Provençal style is complemented by the simple design of the lamp, with an industrial form finished in translucent glass.

Different light sources for the various areas in the kitchen. For the cooking area, the incorporation of a lamp in the extractor hood is the most versatile and attractive solution as an independent light would need constant cleaning and maintenance.
The table for informal meetings only requires general lighting, in this case provided by two stainless steel lamps hanging over the ends of the table.

Light around the bed

In the bedroom it must be possible to turn the lights on and off from the bedhead, and so the switches must be within reach. It is advisable to reinforce the bed light with general illumination, either from lamps with shades or spotlights on the ceiling. The reading light should be sharply focused and equipped with an articulated arm.

Two wall lamps with extendable arms light up the bedhead. The contrast between the subdued decoration and the upholstery of the bed provides a very well balanced finish.

The decoration in this room, with an obvious classic inspiration, has been carried out in colors that go well together. The subdued lighting makes the white of the bed and canopy stand out, giving them greater prominence.

Creative use of space. A room to fulfill the double function of bed and living area. The reverse side of the headboard serves as a cupboard, while the lamp completes the overall effect.

The blue wall uses contrasts to create an illusion of depth. The distinctive form of the piece of furniture at the bedhead provides the basis for the decorative solution of asymmetrical lighting.

Large bedroom where the lighting is distributed by areas. One light for the bedhead and two lamps hanging in one corner combine, with their paper shades, to create a soft illumination.

Purity of form for a bedroom with a modern look. The general lighting is complemented by a standard lamp and two halogens on the ceiling that throw light on the bedhead.

Lighting in the bathroom

The traditional distribution of the home assigns the bathroom to an inner room starved of sunlight. If it does have windows, these are usually small and admit little or no light, and so artificial lighting becomes a basic requirement for the bathroom. It is a good idea to combine directional light sources for the most important areas with a more general lighting scheme to achieve a more balanced and serene effect.

The general lighting in this bathroom comes from the two halogen spotlights set into the ceiling.

Two wall lamps with articulated arms confer a classic touch on the bathroom. The blue tiles also brighten up the space.

Two cone-shaped wall lamps are responsible for lighting the sink area in this bathroom. The lamps form a symmetrical pattern with the mirrors.

The main feature of the lighting is a wall lamp with a functional and modern finish.

The rustic decorative style aims to create an environment that conveys the simplicity and tranquillity of country life. However, in the bathroom the rustic style can permit the introduction of modern stainless steel elements. The lighting in this space has been achieved with halogen lights that throw their light on the pale-colored panels.

The subdued lighting resulting from halogens on the ceiling seeks to play with the reflections produced in this bathroom built entirely of marble.

A small bathroom needs to resort to various decorative results to make it seem bigger. The two mirrors here intensify the vertical light emitted by the wall lamp.

A very dynamic composition that combines a rustic-style roof with a sharply defined shower cubicle. The general lighting emanates from the beams and is reflected in the spaces between them to produce a highly original effect.

The Art Deco influence distinguishes this bathroom lit by two antique wall lamps.

Original placement for a wall lamp with a classic touch. This type of lamp, which directs the light upward, produces a very attractive effect.

Various points of light from halogens set into the ceiling are complemented by a neon light placed over the mirror in the area that needs most light.

The color of the lighting is an important factor when undertaking a decoration in various shades. In this bathroom the white light of the halogens enhances the personality of the setting.

Romantic setting with a self-evident classic inspiration. The wall lamps with articulated arms give all the light required, thanks to the reflections from the pale colors of the decoration.

When a bathroom is dominated by pale colors the lighting is better distributed as it reaches every corner, and there is no need for direct light from wall lamps.

The shades of ocher make this setting very cozy. The lighting in this bathroom produces a very intimate effect.

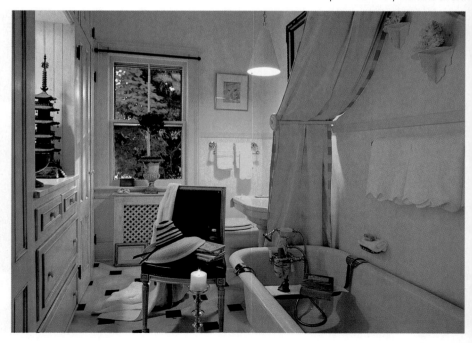

Industrial designs

The evergreen tendency to look to designs from the past for inspiration has given rise to a style of lamps reminiscent of the lights used in factories in the mid-twentieth century. Their versatile structure means that they can be used in an endless number of permutations, thanks to the flexibility of modern materials. Steel, aluminum, glass, and plastic are the raw materials for a perfect solution to the problem of general lighting, in any setting or style.

Modern lamp made in steel. The austerity of industrial-style design has enabled designers to update and reinterpret these lamps as fashion demands.

Two views of different settings in the home, lit with the same designs, illustrate the decorative versatility of this type of lamp. Their lack of any ornamentation, their rational functionality, and their technical simplicity are the main reasons why these lamps have become so popular in domestic lighting. Both settings are by Besana.

Lamps inspired by industry, under a roof that leaves its architectural structure exposed, heighten the special character of this home.

Another of the possibilities offered by industrial design is that of installing a series of identical pieces without overwhelming a space. The flexibility of the materials used to make these lamps allows a single design to be reproduced in various sizes to suit the purpose.

The great range of possibilities as regards the color and shape of industrial-style lamps means that they can fit into any setting.

Designer lamps

J. Hoffmann (1900).

W. Wagenfeld (1926).

Anónimo (1929).

Anónimo (1930).

W. Wagenfeld (1928).

W. Wagenfeld (1924).

W. Wagenfeld (1924).

W. Wagenfeld (1924).

W. Wagenfeld (1926).

W. Wagenfeld (1928).

Anónimo (1930).

Anónimo (1925).

E. Muthésius (1927).

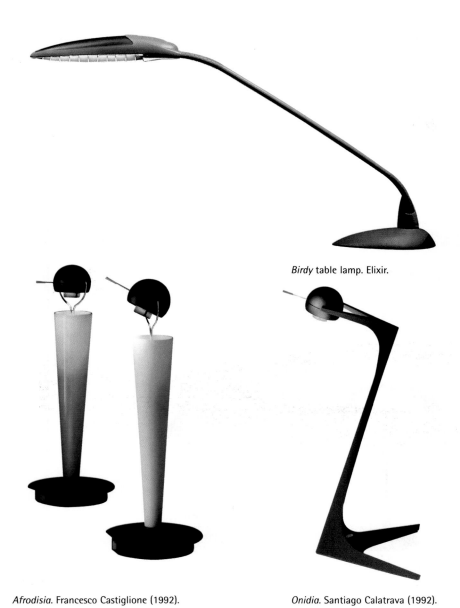

Birdy table lamp. Elixir.

Afrodisia. Francesco Castiglione (1992).

Onidia. Santiago Calatrava (1992).

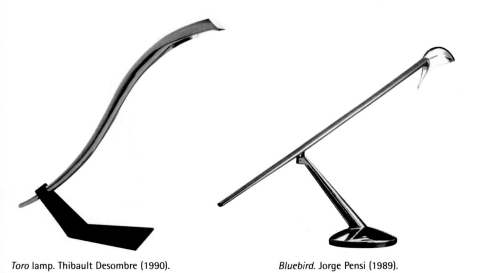

Toro lamp. Thibault Desombre (1990).

Bluebird. Jorge Pensi (1989).

Rodope. Zed (1996).

Mandraki Tavolo. Riccardo Blumer (1996).

Paco. Rodolfo Dordoni (1996).

Oci. Rodolfo Dordoni (1996).

Villa Giulia. Michael Graves (1992).

Profilo lamp. Sergio Cappelli & Patricia Ranzo (1991).

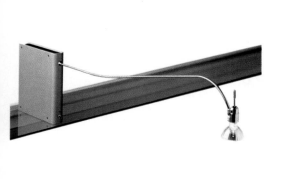

Bib Luz Libro Oscar Busquets.

Brera hanging light. Achille Castiglioni (1992).

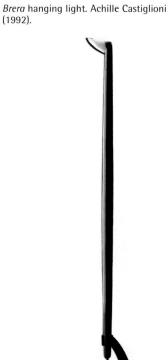

Mezzachimera. Vico Magistretti (1970).

Brera standard lamp. Achille Castiglioni (1992).

Io. Tobias Grau (1990).

Arcadia Tavolo. Ernesto Gismondi &
Giancarlo Fassina (1995).

Miconos Tavolo.
Ernesto Gismondi (1998).

Oblio.
Ernesto Gismondi (1998).

Aggregeto Stelo Tavolo. Enzo Mari
& Giancarlo Fassina (1976).

G.T. Rietveld (1925).

Gilda, In Suk il &
Silvia Capponi (1993).

Zen. D & D Desing (1989).

Shogun Tavolo. Mario Botta (1986).

Frankfurt lamp. Associate Designers (1989).

Galetea Tavolo. Andrea Anastasio (1998).

Soleil Blanc. Didier la Mache.

Cina hanging lamp. Rodolfo Dordoni (1996).

Bolonia. Josep Lluscá.

Kallisto. Tobias Grau (1990).

Amatinte. Agnoletto & Rusconi.

Don Quixote. Ingo Maurer (1989).

Scaragoo. Ingo Maurer & Stefan Lindfors (1989).

Elipse. J.M. Magen.

Creature lamp. Sergio Calatroni (1989).

Tocatta wall lamp. Elmecker & Reuter (1991)

Flic Flac wall lamp. Elmecker & Reuter (1991).

Indor wall lamp. Elmecker & Reuter (1991).

Mephisto wall lamp. Tobias Grau (1990).

Balart. Jorge Pensi.

Atalaya. wall lamp. Josep Joan Teruel (1990).

Vulcano wall lamp. D & D Design. (1989).

Enea. Antonio Citterio (1998).

Artur. Tobias Grau.

Hanging lamps

Fenice 15. Renato Toso, Nati Masari & Ass.

Gaia Rosa. hanging lamp. Örni Hallowen.

Ermione hanging lamp. Örni Hallowen.

Cigno. Örni Hallowen.

Leda Acquamare. Artemide.

Medusa Rubino hanging lamp. Silvio Zanon, Olga Barmine, & Paolo Creapan.

Pantalica Blu. hanging lamp. Örni Hallowen.

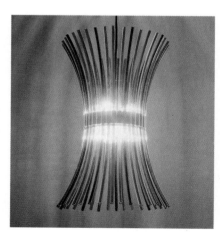

Tamiri Multicolored hanging lamp. Artemide.

Arpasia 40. ceiling lamp. Valery Jean-Marie.

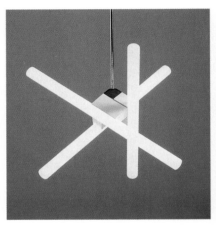

Olvidada. Pepe Cortes.

Arpasia 40. hanging lamp. Artemide.

Doremi' hanging lamp. Jeannot Cerutti.

Gitana. hanging lamp. Jeannot Cerutti.

Vega 70 hanging lamp. Artemide.

Ilias. Andrea Anastasio.

Zsu-Zsu hanging lamp. Örni Hallowen.

Wall and ceiling lamps

Zsu-Zsu ceiling lamp.
Örni Hallowen.

Pull. Claudio
Marturano.

Roby. Artemide.

Spider. Jeannot
Cerutti.

Rebeca ceiling lamp.
Studio Veart.

Doremi' ceiling lamp.
Jeannot Cerutti.

Amanita. Umberto
Riva.

Goccia. Studio Veart.

Prima. Giuseppe
Righetto.

Iole ceiling lamp.
Ernesto Gismonti &
Giancarlo Fesina.

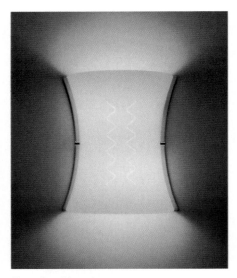

Fama. Toso Massari e
Associati.

Robbia 60, Robbia 30.
Ennio Pasini.

Cilla. Ernesto
Gismondi.

Vesta Full. Ernesto
Gismondi &
Giancarlo Fesina.

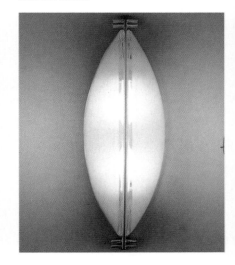

Masha wall lamp.
Jeannot Cerutti.

Arpasia wall lamp.
Valery Jean-Marie.

Vesta. Ernesto
Gismondi & Giancarlo
Fesina.

Bubbola.
Umberto Riva.

Gitana wall
lamp. Jeannot
Cerutti.

Boli. Artemide.

Nausicaa 12.
Masimo Giacan.

Nausicaa 18.
Masimo Giacan.

Antea. Ernesto
Gismondi.

Mask. Ennio Pasini.

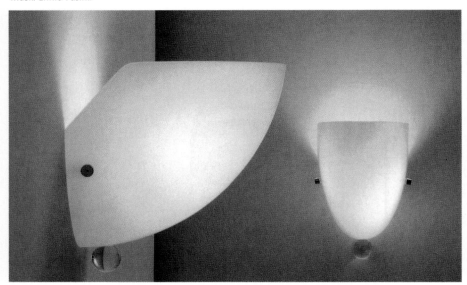

Lighting for the table

Coppa. Jeannot Cerutti.

Iole table lamp. Ernesto Gismondi & Giancarlo Fesina.

Ifigenia Priomo. Toni Cordero.

Arpasia table lamp. Valery Jean-Marie.

Toma. Elmar Thome.

Arpasia Luminator. Valery Jean-Marie.

Iole table lamp. Jeannot Cerutti.

Cuma table lamp. Ugo La Pietra.

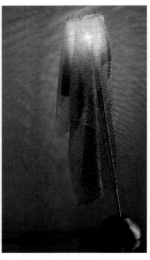

Ecate Anchise Toni Cordero.

Manelao Notte Bianca. Ernesto Gismondi.

Masha table lamp. Jeannot Cerutti.

Cibele. Andrea Anastasio.

Mirra table lamp. Andrea Anastasio.

Iskra. Jeannot Cerutti.

City. Studio Veart.

Otta. Alessandro Mendini.

Standard lamps

Afna. Jeannot Cerutti.

Line. Jeannot Cerutti.

Iole. standard lamp. Ernesto Gismonti & Giancarlo Fesina.

Arpasia. Valery Jean-Marie.　　　　*Auryn.* R.Fusi, S. Mollica, P. Zanotto.　　　　*Acquarelli.* Artemide.

Color

Color plays a decisive role in decoration. Before coming to any decision about specific colors, we have to examine the way we perceive them. This is where light comes into play. Natural light illuminates our home for the greater part of the time. It breathes life into interiors, modifies their tones over the course of the day, and varies with the seasons. This means that we should study the layout of each setting and determine the direction of the light that comes in through the windows and doors, and then try to make the most of it for our decoration.

Northern light is cold and there are few variations in the shadows it throws. If a room faces north, it is best to decorate it with warm colors to counteract any harshness induced by the light. In contrast, southern light gives the impression of warmth and changes direction during the day; cold colors will help to offset any excessive brilliance, especially in summer. Eastern light is the first to appear in the morning, before gradually losing its intensity and becoming more neutral. If a room has a westerly aspect, we may need to shade the sunlight in the late afternoon. Colors can help us to mitigate the effects of light, in conjunction with blinds and drapes.

The cold colors range from blue to green, whilst the warm ones run from yellow to red. The points mentioned above are fundamental when we decide on the colors for the furniture, walls, and floors of the rooms, but another important factor is our own taste and the effect we want to create with color. These days the fashion is to use subtle shades of gray, beige, and dun. However, more adventurous souls can indulge in furniture in vivid breezy colors — the primary colors of red, blue, and yellow in their purest states, and also green. If we are more conservative and shrink at the thought of a red lounge, we can always create a space in softer tones and add touches of color with details such as a lamp or some pictures. The chromatic harmony of a room depends on all the elements in it, from the walls and furniture to the smallest accessory.

Color is not a secondary consideration, it defines the style of a room. If we are aiming to create a bright and relaxing space that will not look dated straight away, the safest bet is beige. Pale colors reflect the light and disperse it around the room. If we are looking for warmth rather than luminosity, yellow is the appropriate color. This color has the ability to make the coldest of spaces seem welcoming. Moreover, it blends very well with blue, ocher, pink, saffron, and mustard. If we want to open out a space visually and conjure up a luminous but unassuming atmosphere, we should opt for blue. To counteract its coldness we can combine it with furniture in natural fibers or add accessories in neutral tones. The most daring among us can choose the remaining primary color — red. It represents the ultimate in warm colors and it is the one that most arouses our senses. Red brings warmth and vitality into our home. If it is combined with shades of ocher it gives rise to a room that is intimate, lively, and very trendy.

Color can also be applied to the floors, but they must fit in with the predominant color in the room. Dark colors make the room seem small, whilst pale ones heighten the impression of space. The floor can also be a stage for more traditional techniques, such as hand-painted tiles. We should let our imagination take wing. The walls, for example, do not only admit paint; we can also finish them with textiles. Paintings and stripes are two options that never go out of fashion. However, it is important to choose fabrics and shades that will maintain our interest.

The chromatic range

Color impinges on proportions, modifies perspectives, regulates the impression of warmth in a setting, and exerts an influence on our state of mind. The chromatic circle enables us to understand particular combinations. Warm colors are those in the sections ranging from violet-red to yellow. The others are cold colors that give a sense of distance and an impression of greater space than there actually is.

The overall effect must be taken into account when choosing the most appropriate color.

Cold and warm colors combine to create relaxed young-looking ensembles. *New York* model by Cicsa.

Colors on opposite sides of the color wheel, like black and white, create contrasts of great elegance. B & B Italia.

Cold colors blend completely with shades of beige and cream to create a neutral cadence.

A feeling of warmth can be obtained by highlighting the appropriate colors.

Cold colors give
a feeling of
distance and
are ideal for
small spaces.

A splash of red gives an original
touch to this armchair, which is
topped off by a metal footrest.

Contrasts and treatments

No color exists in isolation in decoration. It is always affected by its surroundings, be they other colors or light and shade. Light affects the shade, clarity, and warmth of the color.

Plastic chairs with metal legs in various colors. Design by Lamm for Roger sin Roca.

The warm tones of the wood recreate rustic styles in city settings to perfection.

Light creates contrasts in a bedroom dressed in black and untreated textiles.

Net drapes filter the sunlight and modify the colors and shades in the bedroom.

The gleam of the wood catches the eye in an area lit by a large paned window.

The basic color scheme

Combination is another element in the basic color scheme. Just as there is a monochromatic scheme that uses shades of a single color, there are also harmonic and complementary schemes. Analogous harmonic schemes apply the colors next to the main color in the chromatic circle, whilst complementary ones opt for colors on the other side of the circle.

Harmonic schemes offer very decorative and elegant results.

Adjacent shades of cream have been applied in this attic, with touches of colors from the opposite side of the color wheel, like green, to provide contrasts.

A palette of cold colors has been chosen to decorate this child's bedroom. Its astute combinations have resulted in a cheerful, informal area.

Different color schemes can be used to separate spaces within a home.

The contrasts in this bedroom are derived from the white and burgundy colors.

Understanding colors and shades

There are some colors that attract and others that repel, and so the shade of color chosen is one of the determining factors in decoration, along with texture and light. The addition of a brightly colored linoleum floor or a discreetly shaded carpet radically alters the appearance of a snow-white room. The proportions are the same but the setting's response to light varies with the change in color and material.

Different shades of wood create beautiful decorative effects.

Metal finishings achieve tones that unify a modern bedroom.

The various shades within a wide range of cold blues and grays fully integrate the stainless steel fittings with the accessories.

Decorating with blues

Blue always evokes open spaces and is associated with peace and quiet. It was not introduced into painting until the end of the Middle Ages, when sky blue replaced gold as a symbol of divinity. It is a perfect choice for children's bedrooms and creates striking decorative effects when combined with warm yellow colors.

View of a bedroom painted pale blue. The tapestry by Joan Miró creates beautiful contrasts.

Intense electric blues are often used in modern decorations. Here the tone is intensified by the light pouring in through the skylight.

Corridor in the *Villa Escarrer* in Palma de Mallorca, designed by Martorell & Bohigas & Mackay. Motifs applied by hand stand out against the blue background.

Yellows

Yellows also give an impression of light and warmth. Three main groups can be distinguished within the scale of this color: subdued yellows or creams, lemon yellows, and intense yellows.

Intense yellow is a perfect complement for areas painted white, such as the adjacent walls in this bedroom.

Sunlight falls directly onto these walls decorated in a shade of pale yellow.

The white of the textiles takes on an attractive yellowish hue, thanks to the tone of the lights set into the ceiling.

Two-seater couch with cotton upholstery and casters. *Santiago* model from KA International.

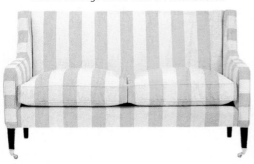

The scale of reds

Red is the color with the longest wavelength and the first in the spectrum that can be distinguished by the naked eye. It has a powerful impact, but when used in intelligent combinations it conveys a feeling of comfort and warmth. Red is rarely found in its pure form, either in architecture or decoration.

Venetian stucco in a red verging on orange. Contrast is supplied by the wooden parquet.

The red counterpane breaks the monotony of this child's bedroom.

Double view of the staircase. The light creates a beautiful pearly effect on this orange-colored wall.

Opposite: The entrance to this house has been painted a fire-red color to transmit the greatest possible feeling of welcoming warmth, and to contrast with the metal of the grille and the terracotta on the floor.

Decorating with whit

White is the color of movement; it is quintessential to modern design and architecture and was frequently used by seminal figures such as Le Corbusier and Walter Gropius. White can conjure up an effect of bright open space that fits in well with yellow, blue, gray, and black.

View of the lounge and dining room of the *Harding Township House* in New Jersey, designed by Richard Meier, with striking combinations of white and neutral tones.

The white walls reflect the light and heighten the sense of place in this exterior. The green of the tree provides a splash of color.

Bathroom decorated in black and white, with touches of warmth supplied by the wood. *Ann* model from Ikea.

Richard Meier applies a white finish to all his work, and this can be attractively set off by black furniture and accessories.

Shades of gray

Gray seems something indefinite, perhaps because it is a halfway point between black and white. It is an unstable and diffuse color, ideal for avant-garde minimalist decorations as it combines effortlessly not only with black and white but also with metal finishes.

The gray marble of the walls creates watery effects that gleam in the sunlight streaming through the small window.

Dining room in the *Kidosaki House* by Tadao Ando. The architect has almost entirely dispensed with color and creates a decoration in which the interplay of light and shade plays a crucial role. In Japan gray has metaphysical overtones and is associated with silence.

The wooden structure takes on a grayish hue, thanks to the light entering through the high windows. This is complemented by the gray of the floor.

The steel surfaces give a feeling of space, as in this kitchen.

A spectacular setting decorated in metallic gray. This color is heightened by the metal accessories, chairs, and turned legs of the glasstop table.

Textiles and color

Upholstery and drapes can provide decisive touches of color in any setting. When choosing fabrics it is important to consider factors such as the light and the aspect of the room and the overall style of the home.

Yellow fabrics endow the setting with warmth and cheerful light.

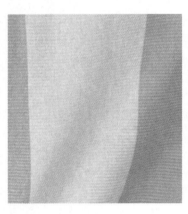

Baykal. K.A Internacional.

Augusta Amarilla. from KA International.

Baykal Rombos. K.A. Internacional.

Mármara Dorado, K.A. Internacional.

Setting in which greens and
reds have been combined.

Ródano Mostaza. K.A.
Internacional.

Garona Mostaza. K.A.
Internacional.

Dorset Verde. K.A.
Internacional.

Elite Verde Hoja. K.A.
Internacional.

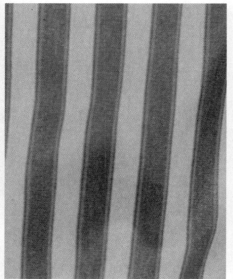

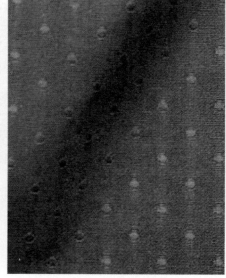

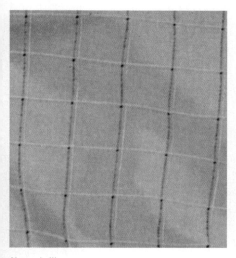

Natural silk.

Malta Gris.

Bahía. *Mieres Beige.*

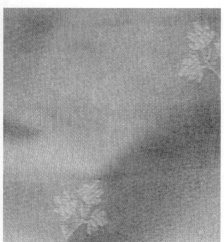

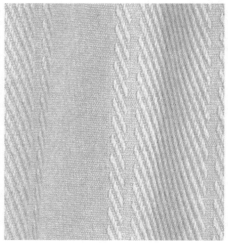

The rough hues of the upholstery on the armchairs contrast with the wood of the chair and the setting's structural elements.

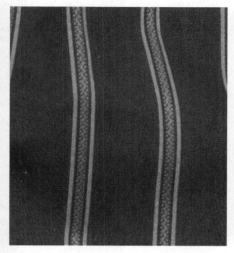

Dallas Rojo.

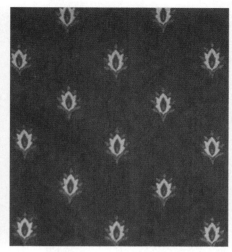

Garona Rojo-Dorado.

Peñiscola Roja. *Cardiff Rojo.*

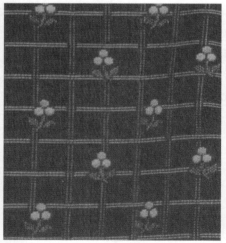

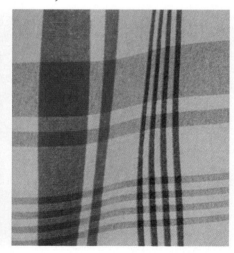

The red of the drapes provides an effective contrast to the white in this functional modern bathroom.

Bristol Azul.

San Diego Azul.

Libia Azul.   *Chenilla Lisa.*

The combination of blues
bestows elegance and
tranquillity on a rustic kitchen.

Mixing colors

To conclude this chapter devoted to color, some thought is given to different examples of decoration based on combinations of colors. In fact, the essence of decoration is the combination of furniture, fabrics, and colors, and the settings chosen offer an exciting glimpse of the wide range of possibilities. They are original and brightly colored, although they will not be to everyone's taste.

A perfect illustration of color combination. This façade clearly follows the South American colorist tradition established by Barragan.

A small room for the telephone features various colors and materials. It also incorporates decorative symbols inspired by letters and numbers.

The bathroom can also be the object of eclectic decoration, thereby giving it a character closer to that of the other rooms in the home.

This lounge revels in combinations of colors – not only on the walls,
ceiling and furniture, but also on the lighting elements, the
covering of the pillars, and the finishing materials.

Design by country

Design is never gratuitous or innocent. It has its roots in the personality of an artist, and in the cultural heritage and distinguishing traits of the place in which he or she is born. So we shall survey the stylistic trends of some of the countries that are most representative of the last hundred years.

Whereas in the nineteenth century Portuguese art was in the doldrums and its architecture had to look to the past for inspiration, in the twentieth century the situation altered radically. Portuguese architecture benefited from a period of progress in which it adopted the latest trends; in design, we cannot speak of one style definitive of Portugal, but of several: the ironic, the architectural, the sculptural, and the minimalist.

As regards Germany, the influence of the Belgian Henri van de Velde and the Austrian J. M. Olbrich led to a great stylistic liberty in the fields of architecture and decoration. The buildings of Peter Behrens marked the beginnings of rationalist architecture, which Walter Gropius, Eric Mendelsohn, and Mies van der Rohe — all members of the Bauhaus — took to its peak. Today, Germany still has a taste for simplicity of form and purity of line, but also relishes details that endow its designs with great beauty.

Austria is currently one of the most innovative countries in the field of design. At the beginning of the twentieth century, the Vienna Secession emerged as a reaction to Art Nouveau and advocated the fusion of art and design — even then, the supremacy of design was being proclaimed. Nowadays, Austrian design searches for objects stripped down to their most basic forms invests in experimentation and the quest for new ideas.

The Netherlands still owes much of its design to the movement that grew up at the beginning of the twentieth century around the "De Stijl" magazine: Neoplasticism. The reduction of forms to their basic lines and the use of primary colors are its main characteristics. There has recently been a revival in this practical style, in which nothing is superfluous. The furniture has well defined geometrical forms and its simple lines are plain to see.

Belgium was home to one of the key artistic events at the end of the nineteenth century, the birth of "Les Vingt", a group of avant-garde artists who sought to take over the reins of French Impressionism. It is not clear what links this group had with Victor Horta, but the latter's crucial role in the Belgian architecture of this period is beyond doubt. Horta was the standard bearer of Art Nouveau and his interiors were distinguished by their combination of functionality and creativity. Even at the turn of the nineteenth century technical innovation was highly regarded, and these days there is a similar emphasis on technological development allied with comfort and visual harmony. Belgian design seeks beauty in minimalism.

In Norway there were two distinct architectural schools in the twentieth century: one advocated a return to tradition, albeit along modern lines, while the other sought inspiration in modern European architecture. These two trends were united, under the influence of Asplund, Gropius, and Le Corbusier, and gave rise to an architecture that upheld traditional features whilst adapting them to environmental and social circumstances. Nowadays there are also two main tendencies in Norway: one gives priority to functionality, whilst the other considers design to be of primary importance.

Swedish design, on the other hand, is not rife with internal divisions. It is wholeheartedly committed to functionalism and minimalism. It does not require any superficial adornment and favors basic geometrical lines, though it does occasionally make way for curves.

In contrast, Canadian design relishes detail and explores the diversity of form and materials. Its products are not tied to any rigid patterns: the only limits are those of the imagination.

In the last ten years of the twentieth century Italian design has developed into Europe's most important style. It is characterized by a variety of forms and the use of many different colors.

Portuguese design

At the beginning of the new millennium Portugal has united all the prevailing trends and ways of understanding design. We can therefore find furniture and objects with an ironic design that overhauls existing models to find new solutions; architectural design, in which materials are treated and combined with a language more akin to architecture; sculptural design, which emphasizes functionality; minimalist design, sparing in the resources it draws upon; and playful design, where the pieces aim to amuse. Portuguese designers also indulge in redesign, involving the revival and updating of classic designs by acknowledged masters, and historical design, which uses traditional materials and objects.

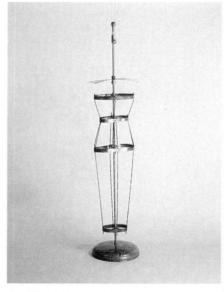

Geraldina clothes horse in iron and steel. Luisa Coder & José Russell. 1999.

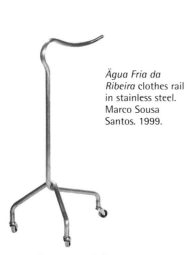

Ägua Fria da Ribeira clothes rail in stainless steel. Marco Sousa Santos. 1999.

Seat Up space divider veneered on both sides in cherry wood and plated in stainless steel.
José Viana. 1999.

Looks lamp in acrylic, lycra, rubber, and nylon. Design by Plácido Alonso, José Luis Ferreira, & Rui Freire.

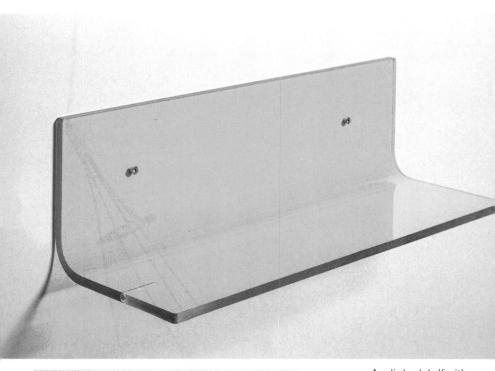

Acrylic bookshelf with rear panel. Fernando Brizio. 1999.

Bergère chair with casters, molded, and veneered on both sides. Daciano Costa. 1999.

2001 umbrella stand in stainless steel, brass, and wood. Adalberto Dias. 1999.

Candeeiro lamp in glass. Eliane Marques.

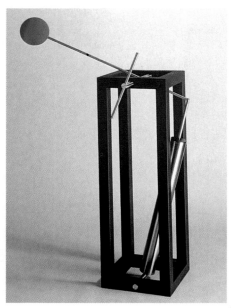

Oscillator in iron, steel, and aluminum. Paulo Vale. 1999.

Steel lamp with mat finish. Design by Gut Moura Guedes. 1999.

Golha showcase in painted steel, designed by Isabel Damaso. 1999.

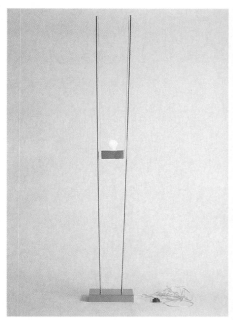

Synthetic foam lamp with inner structure and base in tube coated in painted steel. José Manuel Cravalho Aráujo.

Canadian design

Jean Pierre Viau, Claude Maufette, Jean François Jacques, Christian Bélanger, Jean-Guy Chabauty, Nathalie Morin, and Serge Tardif embody the diversity and originality characteristic of Canadian design, especially in Montreal and Quebec. Their work covers the representative styles in the country, embracing industrial experience, craftsmanship, and a daringly independent attitude to fashion.

Morin lamp.
Tardif Designers.
1995.

Pepperoni stacking table.
Claude Maufette. 1997.

Tania
armchair.
Plouk Design.
1995.

ST-120 chair.
Météore Design. 1991.

Some typical
Canadian designs.

Swedish design

Swedish design is simple and very
functional. Its origins lie in the
nineteenth century, although the
personality that defines it today was
forged between the 1930s and 1950s.
It was in 1930 that its distinguishing
traits began to emerge: functionalism,
simple lines, and pale wood.

Carpet on Carpet
rug. Design by Jonas
Bohlin.

Rug designed by
Kristina Rästrom.

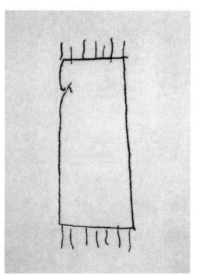

Wooden bathroom furniture.
Designs by E. Koivisto,
O. Rune, and M. Claesson.

Wooden dining
room table,
designed by
Jacques Sanjian.

Lyra armchair. Design by Jonas Bohlin.

Dover chair. Design by Björn Alge.

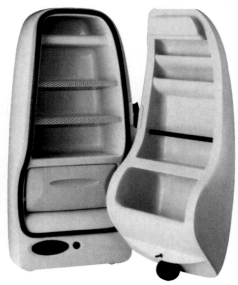

OZ refrigerator from the Electrolux Group.

Osmium lamp
from Ikea.

1301 woolen
rug from
Carouschka.

Dining room table
and chairs, by
Marten Claesson,
Eoro Koivisto, and
Ole Rune.

Three-seater
couch. Ikea.

Austrian design

Austrian design is one of the most advanced in Europe. The objects made in this central European country range from experimental prototypes to short-lived projects and rendered images created by designers such as Christian Horner, Hans Hollein, and Uli Marchsteiner.

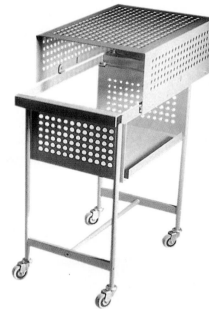

Cadillac trolley, designed by Michael Wagner.

Steamer. Design by Hasenbichler/Hollander.

Wicker couch. Design by Eeos.

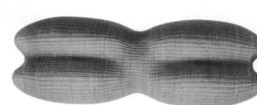

Box designed by
Martin Szekely.

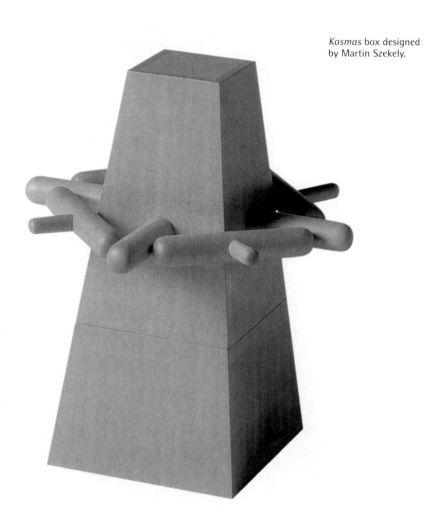

Kosmas box designed
by Martin Szekely.

Mobile office.
Pneumatic construction.
Hans Hollein.

Home office system by Uli
Marchsteiner. Virtual presence.

Packaging in potato
starch, wood shavings,
and pulp. Graz
packaging center.

Belgian design

The roots of Belgian design lie in its combination of functionality, technology, and visual elegance. Their designers' stylized objects, that fulfill their function without any superfluous details that distract them from their essential purpose, can blend into all types of settings. Figures like Ann Maes are typical of the growing trend toward formal minimalism to be seen in Belgian design.

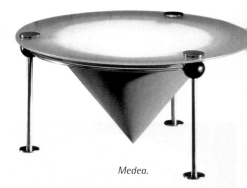

Medea.

Rotonda table and *Tino* chair.

Tondo lights.

Norwegian design

As in the rest of Scandinavia, functionality is the overriding consideration in Norwegian design. However, there is a growing trend to break away from the homogeneity that has built up and put expression and visual appeal above utility.

Shelf unit from Solveig Johnson.

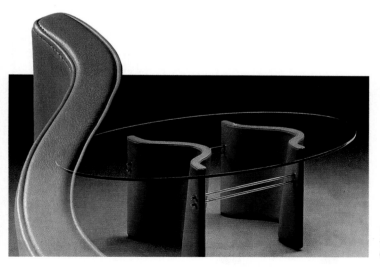

Vatne 245 table. Design by Olav Eldoy.

Chair designed by Espen Arnesen.

Café-Sit chair by Birgitte Appelong.

Chair and stool by Sigurd Strom.

German design

A predilection for natural materials, craftsmanship, and a close attention to detail are some of the distinguishing features of German design. It also favors clarity of line and smooth textures that offer great comfort.

Salomon candelabra.

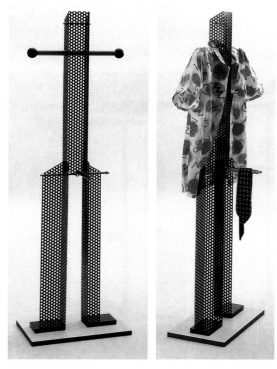

Charles coat stand. Design by Hermann Waldenburg.

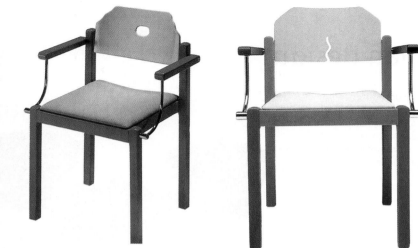

Galopp chairs by
Waldemar Rothe.

Sinus chairs by
Waldemar Rothe.

Italian design

Italian design differs from
Nordic design in that it always
favors a daring use of acid or
pastel colors and a
predominance of sensuous
lines and curves.

Ago2 Treats. Design by
Anna Gili. Alessi. 1998.

Rondo, Otto, Sden, designed by
Stefano Piravono. 1998. Alessi.

King Kong. Stefano Giovannoni
and Guido Venturini. Alessi.

Bedside table and clothes horse, designed by Roberto Giaocomucci. Marchetti. 1999.

Bookmark. Design by Massimo Scolari. 1998. Alessi.

Genetic Tales vase by Andrea Branzi, 1998. Alessi.

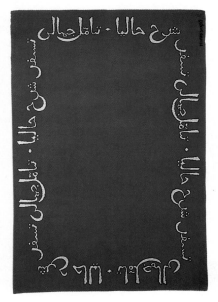

Puig rug by Eduard Samsó.

Spanish design

The 1990s demonstrated that the upsurge in Spanish design was not an ephemeral phase, because it went on to consolidate itself as one of the world leaders, on account of its originality and the quality of its production. André Ricard, Pete Sans, and Javier Mariscal are just some of its designers with an international reputation.

Buck Tensor. Jaume Tresserra.

Fonda Europa side table. Carles Riart.

Facto Mini chair. Gemma Bernal and Ramón Isern.

Troika chair from Carlos Jané Camacho.

Bruja chair. Pete Sans.

Fonda Europa armchair. Carles Riart.

Dutch design

Practicality and sobriety characterize today's
design in the Netherlands. Its international
reputation is derived from leading figures like Jan
de Bouvrie, Henke Voos, and Brickman. Such
artists have a knack of applying esthetic criteria
to objects in everyday use to produce a design
marked by its simplicity of line, its assimilation of
geometric forms inherited from the painter
Mondrian, and a minimalism shared by its Nordic
neighbors. Its latest trends emphasize classic
forms and complement them with chic fabrics.

Pouf upholstered in
corded silk. Design
by Ravage.

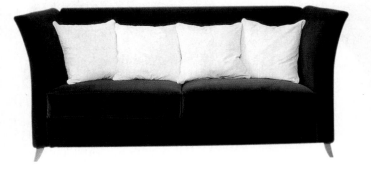

Three-seater
couch with
beech legs
and black
upholstery.
Design by Jan
de Bouvrie.

Small armchair with armrests. *Emperor* model. Design by Ravage.

Original armchair, upholstered in black and with beech legs. *Château* by Jan de Bouvrie.

Ponza is an oval center table with a glass top and wrought iron legs. Design by Maroeska Metz for Arx.

Pouf in corded silk, designed by Maroeska Metz for Arx.

Pouf upholstered in corded silk with a metal base. Design by Maroeska Metz.

Closet-chest of drawers with aluminum handles. Design by Brand 8 van Egmond for Arx.

Suite of couch and armchair upholstered in brown crushed velvet. Design by Brand 8 van Egmond for Arx.

French design

French design seeks a balance between two concepts that often seem irreconcilable: beauty and functionality. All the objects created by French designers are marked by a distinctive national style, characterized by its innate mastery of elegance.

Forme du Voyage lamp by Pascal Morgue.

Louis Vuitton collection, designed by Christian Liagre.

Torito chair. Studio Naço.

Chair by Eric Schmitt.

Ashtray armchair by Eric Schmitt.

Japanese design

Japanese design is characterized by complete decorations almost entirely free of adornment – a minimalism that has exerted a great influence on Western countries. Creative discipline and compositional rigor are other qualities that govern contemporary Japanese design.

Dear Vera table clocks by Shigeru Uchida and Aldo Rossi. 1998.

Standing light. Isao Hosoe.

Dining room in the *Circle House* designed by Naoyaki Shirakawa.

Stormo bookcase.
Isao Hosoe.

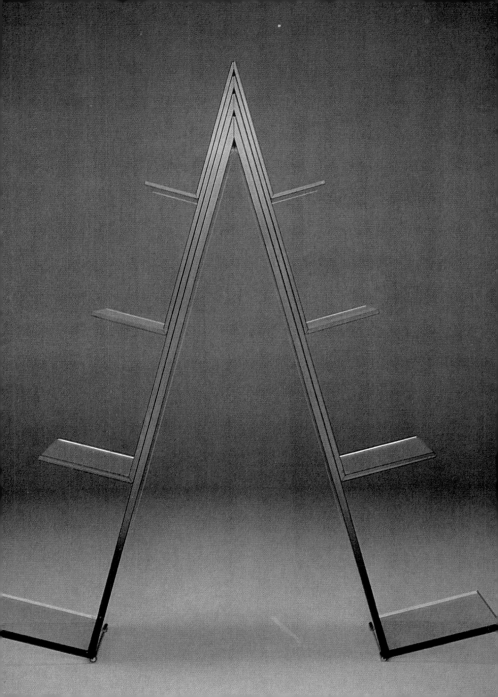

Tonel chair. Frank Lloyd
Wright. 1904–1905.

Tokio Imperial
armchair, designed
by Frank Lloyd
Wright.

Upholstered aluminum
chair. Donald Deskey. 1929.

Pencil sharpener. Raymond Loewy.
1933.

American design

Current American design is characterized by a masterly use and combination of materials, a special attention to volume, and an eminently rationalist artistic equilibrium. Frank Lloyd Wright was the prime mover of this rationalism, whilst Donald Deskey was the motivating force behind the use of alternative materials like cork and steel and the investigation of aerodynamic movement.

A pair of beechwood chairs. Charles & Ray Eames. 1946. Screen by Herman Miller. 1946.

Lamp by Donald Deskey. 1930.

The designers of the twentieth century

Cascanueces. Stefano Giovanni

T he first reaction against the overly decorative style of the early years of the twentieth century can be attributed to the Austrian architect Adolf Loos. His ideas were very modern, if we take into account the fact that today's trends are distinguished by their decorative simplicity. His designs, and his theories on the elimination of superficial ornamentation, inspired what was to become the Modernist movement. Along the same lines, from 1919 the Bauhaus School sought to unite art and industry. One of the groups that most influenced the Bauhaus was the De Stijl, headed by Piet Mondrian, Theo van Doesburg, and the designer Geerrit Rietveld.

Butaca 44. Alvar Aalto.

The De Stijl movement restricted itself to the primary colors, plus black, gray, and white. It favored simple geometrical forms and confined itself to horizontal and vertical planes. Rietveld's "Red-Blue" armchair, built with strips of turned wood, was one of the first works to be created by the De Stijl. Around the same time, the Modernist Le Corbusier threw down a challenge to the elitism of the decorative arts by advocating the need for functional objects for interiors. Le Corbusier's guiding principle was the elimination of all superfluous elements from buildings and interiors and their reduction to basic geometric forms.

The Finnish Modernist Alvar Aalto is well known for the sinuous forms of his furniture, pitchers, and roofs. His love of nature can be seen in the harmonious fusion of his buildings with their environment. However, Aalto did not neglect human needs, and his curved wooden chairs aimed for maximum comfort. This architect and designer had a predilection for wood, a material capable of creating warm and welcoming settings. The influence of Aalto can still be seen today in the work of designers like Rud Thygessen and Johnny Sorensen.

Aparador. Charles R. Mackintos

It was not until the 1960s that the tenets of the Modernist movement began to be challenged (although there were still movements, such as High Tech, that expressed their support). Postmodernism gave form to the rejection of Modernism and produced startling designs aimed at the consumer market. The architect and designer Michael Graves provided landmarks of Postmodernism with his Public Service building in Portland and his furniture for the Italian Memphis Group.

The official support given by the French authorities to Postmodernist designers like Philippe Starck does much to explain their popularity in the 1980s, and their continuing success today. Starck's designs are eminently human; as he says himself, he creates from the heart. His work ranges from easy chairs to coffee pots, and they are all marked by their convenience and by design that oscillates between a return to basics and a truly astonishing originality. He loves using curved shapes and materials like plastic and recycled wood. The premises for his work are sex, humor, politics, and surrealism. One of Starck's former collaborators, the Italian Pierangelo Caramia, also favors functional objects that serve a practical purpose without neglecting the values of good design and craftsmanship.

Design is a total art. It embraces all types of objects, from the most everyday to the most exclusive, from furniture to buildings. However, there are some designers that focus their attention on one specific field. This is the case with Arne Jacobsen, famous for his faucets, which leave visible only the handles and end pipes. Ingo Maurer, on the other hand, has specialized in lighting, constantly seeking new materials and forms. Arnold Merckx has concentrated on the work environment, producing the kind of functional but highly attractive furniture that would be the joy of any corporation — providing, of course, its budget stretches that far.

From Spain one designer has burst on to the international scene with work that never fails to arouse controversy: Javier Mariscal. His drawings are innocent, deliberately childish in fact, but the wide range of furniture and accessories he has designed is astonishingly original. Not as well known, but just as important, is the Catalan André Ricard, who combines his design work with teaching and theoretical texts.

Silla Batlló. Antonio Gaudí.

Alvar Aalto

Born Jyväskylä, 1898; died Helsinki, 1976.
Although his first works as an architect (*Vipuri Library*, 1927-1935; *Paimio Sanatorium*, 1928) followed the lines of the Modernist movement, at the end of the 1930s, with the *Villa Mairea* (1938), he began to create organic buildings that combined different materials, were fragmented, or incorporated curves.

He established himself as a furniture designer in 1935, under the auspices of the Artek Foundation in Helsinki, along with his wife Aino Aalto and Mairea Gullichson. In this period he began to produce pieces, like the stool with three legs, that were remarkably modest but meticulously finished.

Butaca 44, Artek.

A440 lamp. Artek.

900 and *901* trolleys.
Artek.

Taburete 60, Artek.

Ron Arad

Born Tel Aviv, 1951. Arad has been responsible for a wide range of projects in both architecture and design. He has worked extensively for such prestigious firms as Driade, Vitra International, Artemide, Poltrona, and Alessi on designs covering all fields of decoration. He made his name in 1981 with the *Rover* couches, which used leather seats from old automobiles. In 1991 he won huge success for a series of upholstered chairs that dispensed with his customary metal materials. Ron Arad has been Professor of Design at the Royal College of Art in London since 1997.

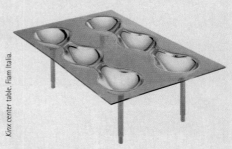

Kinx center table. Fiam Italia.

Onda Corta bedside table, for Fiam Italia.

Soundtrack CD rack. Alessi. 1999.

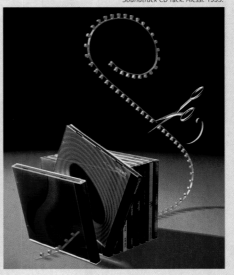

Onda Kart closet. Fiam Italia.

Achille Castiglioni

Born Milan, 1918. Achille Castiglioni studied architecture at the Milan Polytechnic. He graduated in 1944 and immediately started to work for the architect brothers Livio and Pier Giacomo. Livio left the firm in 1952 and Pier died in 1968. Castiglioni developed his career as a designer through his work with companies like Alessi, e De Padova, Flos, Driade, Knoll, Olivetti, BBB Over, and Kartell. He was a professor at Turin Polytechnic from 1970 to 1980, when he started teaching at Milan Polytechnic. According to Castiglioni, the mission of the designer is to investigate and further the functional possibilities of objects in order to improve the quality of life.

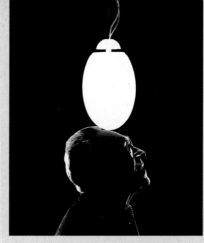

With the *Brera* lamp he designed for Flos.

Tavolo'95. e De Padova.

Stylos. Flos.

Mate. e De Padova.

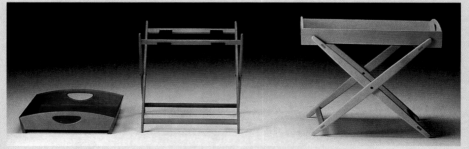

Taraxacum, Flos.

Single-handle mixer with fixed pipe.

Arne Jacobsen designed a series of faucets that won him great acclaim among architects and interior designers. This success was the result of a close collaboration between Jacobsen and the manufacturer Verner Overgraad  for a competition sponsored by the National Bank of Denmark in 1961. It bore fruit in this series of faucets built into the wall, with only the handles and end pipes visible. The Vola company has been marketing them ever since, and their popularity has increased with the years.

Two-handle mixer.

Single-handle mixer with mobile pipe.

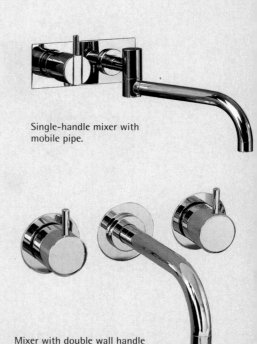

Single-handle mixer with mobile pipe.

Mixer with double wall handle and fixed pipe.

Eero Arnio

Born Helsinki, 1932. Eero Arnio is represented in some of the world's most important museums, such as the Victoria and Albert Museum in London and the Museum of Modern Art in New York. His works include the hanging acrylic *Bubble* chair (1968), the *Serpentina* chair (1968), and the *Screw* and *Copacabana* glass fiber tables (1991). Arnio's creative process is distinguished by its resolution of technical and ergonomic problems, although his work's real importance lies in its visual impact.

Screw, 1991.

Copacabana table. 1991.

Antonio Gaudí

Calvet bench in varnished solid oak, 1902, B.d.

Born Reus, 1852; died Barcelona, 1926. An essential reference point in the history of architecture, Antoni Gaudí also designed furniture from the start of his career and, like other Modernist architects, involved himself in every aspect of the interior design of his buildings. His designs, with their highly personal interpretation of the tenets of Modernism, are extremely organic and clearly draw on forms found in nature.

Calvet chair, 1902, B.d.

Calvet chair, 1902, B.d.

Batlló chair, B.d.

Calvet chair, 1902, B.d.

Iron fittings and door handles, 1902–1910, B.d.

Jean Michel Cornu
Veronique Malcourant

Born Saigon, 1956. Vichy, 1955. Cornu and Malcourant work within the current of Symbolic Design, but their interest in symbolism does not preclude rigor or functionality. They have become leaders in playful design, and have produced some of the most interesting and imaginative work on offer today. Furthermore, their work stands out in their particular field for its resistance, flexibility, and good value.

Odéon. 1989.

Comette collection. 1990.

Comette collection. 1990.

Comette collection. 1990.

Comette collection. 1990.

Eileen Gray

Born Ireland 1878; died 1976. Eileen Gray is, without any doubt, one of the women who has exerted the most influence on modern design. Her search for new forms and materials led to innovative furniture made of exotic or lacquered wood. Particularly outstanding are the *S* chair (1932–1934), with its folding frame and textile seat, and the steel table made in 1927 for the *E.1027 House* in Roquebrune, in the South of France.

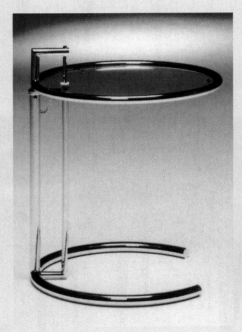

Steel table. Architects.

Lacquered table. Architec

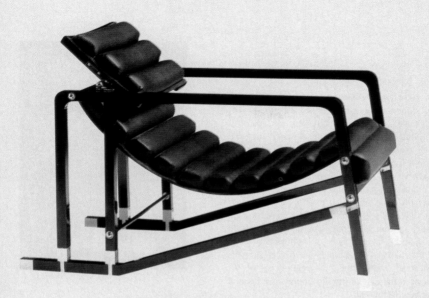

Armchair in leather. Architects.

Folding tables. Architects.

Michael Graves

Born 1934. Michael Graves forms part of a group of designers that emerged in the 1970s. His involvement in the Italian Memphis movement in the 1980s, and the objects he designed for Swid Powell, marked him out as one of the leading figures in contemporary design. Over the course of his extensive career as an architect he has realized over 200 projects, including office blocks, museums, and theaters. He has also been prolific in the field of interior design, producing series of articles for mass production for companies like Arkitektura, Swid Powell, and Baldinger. Some of his objects – *Vajilla Corinto* of 1984, for example – have a certain neo-classical air, whilst others are reminiscent of Art Deco, as in the case of the *Big Dripper* milk jug and sugar bowl from 1986.

Villa Giulia table lamp. Baldinger Architectural Lighting. 1997.

Pendulum clock. Alessi. 1988.

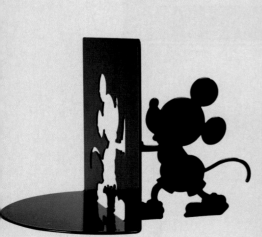

Mickey & Co. is a bookrest. Walt Disney. 1994.

Kettle. Alessi. 1985.

Six-piece kitchen set. Alessi.

Valle cutlery. Alessi. 1994.

Bread tin. 1997.

Cheese plate. Alessi. 1997.

Pepper mill. Alessi. 1988.

Round tray with polyamide handles. 1990.

Round tray. 1991.

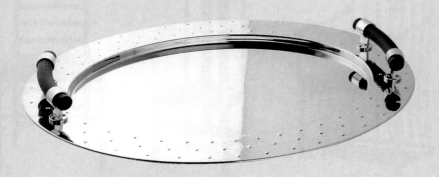

Oval tray with polyamide handles. 1994.

Charles R. Mackintosh

Easy chair. Architects.

Chair. Architects.

Born Glasgow, 1868; died London, 1928.
Architect, representative of the Glasgow School, and one of the founders of Art Nouveau. His highly distinctive furniture designs were particularly outstanding, the elaborate ornamentation of panels and friezes being a constant factor. His most acclaimed furniture was made between 1901 and 1911 for the Glasgow Tea Room and for various private houses. In 1923 he abandoned his career as an architect and began a period devoted to painting that reached its peak in his French and Catalan watercolors. He returned to England in 1927 and died in oblivion the following year.

Chair. Architects.

Chair. Architects.

Chair. Architects.

Chair. Architects.

Domino Table. Bd.

Varnished table. Architects.

Sideboard. Architects.

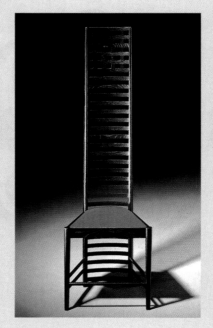

Chair. Architects.

Rud Thygesen
Johnny Sorensen

Born Saeberg, 1932; Helsingor, 1944. This partnership represents one of the most solid bases for design in Denmark today, representative of the latest generation of designers, those strongly influenced by cabinetmaking and figures like Hans J. Wegner and Borge Mogensen. Their designs bear witness to the growing influence of the Klint School of Scandinavian functionalists like Alvar Aalto and Bruno Matthesson. Thygesen and Sorensen work within strict classic parameters to produce pieces that are timeless.

Chair. Magnus Olesen, 1990.

Office chair. Olesen, 1991.

Embassy table. 1989.

Ingo Maurer

Los Minimalos Uno. 1994.

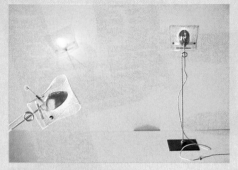

Floatation (1980).

Zero One (1990).

Born Reichenau, Germany, 1932. Maurer studied typography and graphic design in Germany and Switzerland from 1954 to 1958. After working as a freelance designer in the United States for three years, he returned to Germany in 1966 and founded Design M in Munich, which specializes in design for lighting. Ever since his first piece for the company, *Bulb* (on the opposite page, below), Maurer's goal has been the reconciliation of art and industrial design.

Lamp. (1980).

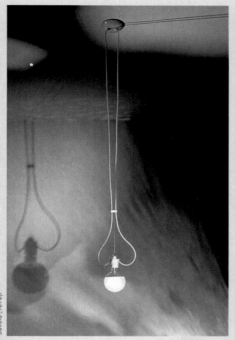

YaYaHo (1984).

Ingo Maurer **875**

Javier Mariscal

Born Valencia, 1950. Since 1977 Mariscal has dedicated himself to graphic art and the creation of a wide range of objects. In 1981 the *Duplex* stool he designed for the bar of the same name in Valencia quickly became a landmark in Spanish design, and Mariscal went on to become one of the most well known designers in the world. His carefree iconoclastic approach transcends his work to become an attitude in itself and constitute a dissenting voice within the world of design.

Alexandre Miró, Juanito Cirici, Pablito Calder y amigos con sal y pimienta en la mesa salt cellars. 1992.

Saula Marina. 1995-1996. Moroso.

Alessandra, 1995-1996.

Ettore Sottsass

Born Innsbruck, 1917. Sottsass, a key figure in design in the second half of the twentieth century, worked extensively in several fields, including painting, pottery, industrial design, and architecture. In the 1960s he developed a very personal language in work for, among others, the Olivetti company – such as a typewriter with a brilliant scarlet structure. His globetrotting gradually led him to distance himself from European rationalism and opt for more elemental designs. He later studied in the Alchimia Studio and created the Memphis Group in 1981. In the early 1990s, Ettore Sottsass started to introduce classic forms and materials into his designs.

La Bella Tavola china. Alessi.

Condiment set. Alessi. 1998.

Butter dish. Alessi. 1998.

Sugar bowls. Alessi. 1998.

Condiment set. Alessi. 1998.

Sugar bowl. Alessi. 1998.

Philippe Starck

Philippe Starck with the *Romeo Moon* lamp.

Born Paris, 1949. Philippe Starck studied in the Nôtre Dame de la Sainte Croix de Neuilly and the École Nissim de Camonde in Paris. He was appointed artistic director for Pierre Cardin at the age of 20. In 1974 he moved to New York, but returned to Paris two years later to design the *Nain Bleu* nightclub. Since then Starck has combined his main activity – industrial and furniture design – with the design of restaurants and hotel interiors and occasional forays into architecture, such as the *La Flamme* and *Naninani* buildings in Tokyo.

Starck has introduced into industrial design the sensuality of early 20th-century sculptors like Arp and Brancusi, the irony of more recent movements, like Pop art and Postmodernism, and the daring of the comic strip. He has become extremely popular as a result.

Hot Bertaa, tetera de Alessi.

Silla Royalton.

Dr. No, Kartell.

Ara, Flos.

Marco Zanuso

Born 1916. Marco Zanuso is one of the most famous Italian post-war designers. Some of his works are now considered classics, and he is one of the pillars of the international success of Italian design. His pieces are characterized by their great originality and simplicity of line; outstanding amongst them are his *Teraillon* kitchen scales (1967) and the *Grillo* folding telephone (1966).

Duna series. 1995.

Duna cutlery. 1995.

Frank Lloyd Wright

Born Wisconsin, 1867; died, Phoenix, 1959. Frank Lloyd Wright personifies the spirit of the pioneers in the American West in the field of architecture. Individualistic, radical, stubborn, nature-loving, Wright invites comparison with Walt Whitman. He designed pieces of furniture for many of his houses, especially those of his Chicago period, that have subsequently been reproduced and marketed commercially. In his furniture he developed a personal graphic language drawing on extremely diverse sources, including the Chicago School, the Arts and Crafts culture, Art Nouveau, the avant-garde, Japanese traditions, and many more. However, as a furniture designer he was not an innovator to the same extent as the architects of the Modernist movement. The pioneer spirit that swelled up in him when he encountered a plot of land was dissipated in his furniture, largely made up of unwieldy geometrical pieces.

Midway 2 chair. Manufactured by Cassina.

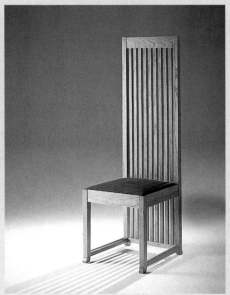

Frank Lloyd Wright **887**

Mies van der Rohe

Born Aquisgran, 1886; died Chicago, 1969. A member of the Bauhaus School, and its director at one point, his furniture designs were inseparable from the functionalist trend toward objects with highly simplified lines, in which the structure of the piece was the determining esthetic factor, avoiding any type of ornamentation. Among his most characteristic designs is the *Barcelona* chair, made to furnish the German pavilion in the 1929 Universal Exhibition, with the steel tubing that set the trend for metal frames. In 1938 he emigrated to the United States, where he went on to become a professor in the Armour Institute in Chicago.

Pouf in leather. Architect.

Pouf in leather. Architect.

Chair with steel frame. Architect.

Easy chair in steel. Architect.

Chair with steel frame. Architect.

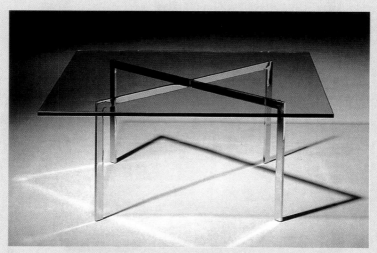

Table with steel frame.

Salvador Dalí

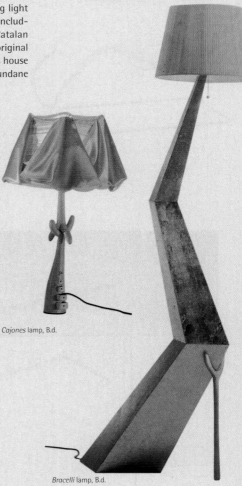

Born Figueres, 1904; died Figueres, 1989.
Salvador Dalí's close friendship with the famous
interior designer Jean Michel Frank, a leading light
of 1930s Paris, led to several joint projects, including the production of furniture. The Catalan
painter's creations included a series of very original
pieces , such as the outdoor furniture for his house
in Port Lligat, but he also designed more mundane
items, such as handles and faucets.

Cajones lamp, B.d.

Muletas lamp, B.d.

Bracelli lamp, B.d.

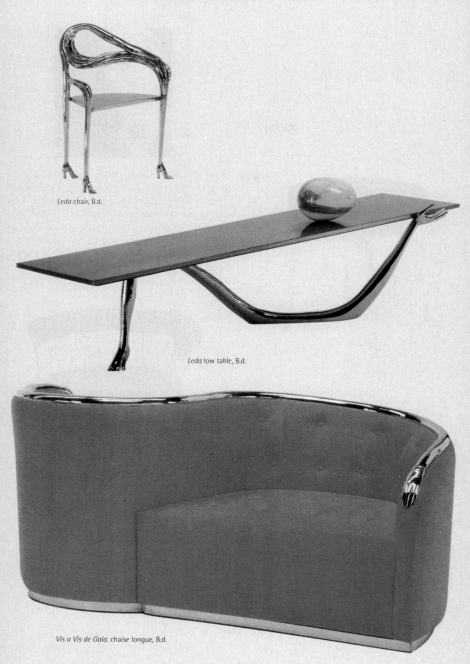

Leda chair, B.d.

Leda low table, B.d.

Vis a Vis de Gala. chaise longue, B.d.

Le Corbusier

Stool. Architects.

Born Chaux de Fonds, 1887; died Roquebrune–Cap Martin, 1965. Le Corbusier introduced functionalism into design and was one of the pioneers in the use of chromed aluminum as a material for construction. His furniture designs use simple open forms and eliminate any decorative element that is not derived from the structure of the piece itself.

Chair. Architects.

Chair. Architects.

Couch. Architects.

Armchair. Architects.

Armchair. Architects.

Couch. Architects.

Richard Sapper

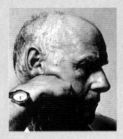

Born 1932. Of all the designers that emerged in the 1970s, Richard Sapper is one of the most respected. He has succeeded in fusing the German rationalist tradition with the experimentation and elegance of Italian design. In 1957 he moved to Milan, where he worked in the studio of Giò Ponti and Alberto Rosselli, and in 1971 he collaborated with Marco Zanuso on the Italian exhibition organized by the Museum of Modern Art in New York. Zanuso has exerted a strong influence on his work, and they have worked together on the design of several audiovisual units. In 1972 he created one of his most well known designs, the *Tizio* lamp, ideally suited to minimalist settings. Richard Sapper now works for companies like Alessi, and he has become a leading figure in industrial design.

RSol cutlery. Alessi. 1995.

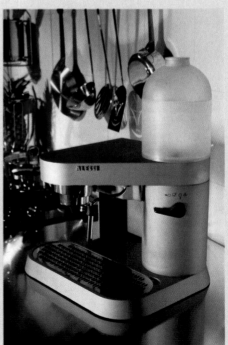

Bandung teapot. Alessi. 1995.

Coban coffee pot, Mono version. Alessi. 1998.

My Beautiful China dinnerware. Alessi.

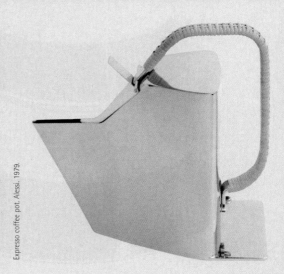

Expresso coffee pot. Alessi. 1979.

Set of three stacking trays. Alessi.

Cooking equipment. Alessi. 1986.

Alessandro Mendini

Born 1931. Alessandro Mendini studied architecture at Milan Polytechnic and went on to join the Studio Nizzoli Associati. In 1978 and 1979 he created "redesign" furniture, such as the *Kandissi* couch and the *Proust* armchair. He is the founder of the Studio Alchimia, and he is considered one of the greatest thinkers and ideologists in contemporary European design. A man of many talents, Mendini has also edited magazines such as *Casabella, Modo* and *Ollo*.

Plate and underplate. Alessi.

Falstaff saucepan with handles. Alessi. 1989.

China. Alessi. 1996.

Anna Time timer. Alessi.

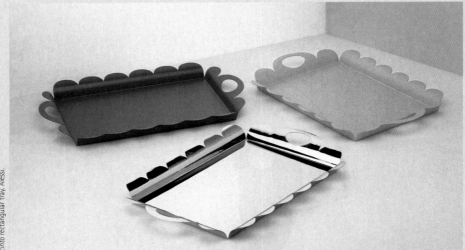

Enzo Mari

Born Novara, 1932. An Italian visual artist and designer, he began his career with a range of experimental kinetic works. In 1952 he began publishing a succession of theoretical texts, and since 1956 he has designed pieces for companies such as Driade and Danese, particularly tiles, textiles, household accessories, and toys. The *Delfina* chair that he designed for Driade in 1974 earned him the Compasso d'Oro award.

Spade. Alessi. 1999.

Spade and accessories. Alessi. 1999.

Ecolo. Alessi.

Ecolo. Alessi.

Trolley in smelted aluminum. Alessi. 1989.

Colander. Alessi. 1997.

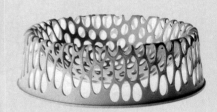

Bread basket. 1997.

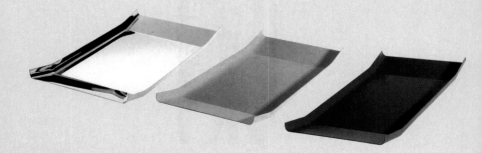

Fruit bowl. Alessi. 1997.

Jasper Morrison

Born 1959. Jasper Morrison's work is characterized by the modesty and boldness with which he interprets design. His objects are eminently practical but are graced with elegant lines. Morrison's minimalist pieces have created a world that discreetly evokes the past. An expert on manufacturing processes, he began to study furniture design in Great Britain, and his *Handlebar* table (1981) was already on the market before he had graduated. His subsequent designs, such as the *Landry Bax* chair, made of strong cardboard and bolts, and the simple plastic wine racks for Magis, represented great innovations – on account of their originality and simplicity.

Pépé le Moko salt cellar. Alessi. 1998.

Round tray table. Alessi. 1998.

Tin Family kitchen tins. Alessi. 1998.

Sim salad servers in PMMA. Alessi. 1998.

Alvaro Siza Vieira

Born Matosinhos, Portugal, 1933. Alvaro Siza Vieira is the foremost exponent of Portuguese architecture, and he has won awards such as the Van der Rohe Architecture Prize and the Putzker Prize. The functionality and esthetic rigor of his designs for furniture, objects, and accessories have won him international acclaim.

Boa Nova couch. 1956.

Mare table and chair. 1997.

Articulated chairs.

Chest of drawers. 1985.

Havana ashtray. 1994.

Faqueiro. 1993–1997.

Glass jars. 1995.

Fruit bowl. 1996.

Andrea Branzi

Born 1938. Andrea Branzi, the founder of the Archizoom Group, is a prominent exponent of radical design, and an important theorist who has published articles in many magazines, such as *Casabella*. His career has included work for Alchimia and Memphis, among others. Very conscious of ecology and natural forms, Branzi always tries to reflect a social and cultural function in his work, and he has a rare sensitivity when bringing objects to life. His passion for genealogy led him to create the book *Genetic Tales*, a compendium and catalog of all the types of men in existence at the beginning of the millennium. His studio was also responsible for a family of objects created for Alessi.

Nutcracker. Alessi. 1999.

Corkscrew. Alessi. 1991.

Bottle opener. Alessi. 1999.

Toothpick holder. Alessi. 1991.

Vase. Alessi. 1998.

Genetic Tales tray. Alessi. 1998.

Mama-ò kettle. Alessi. 1992.

Stefano Giovannoni

One of the leading designers of our times, Stefano Giovannoni always works under the so-called "affective codes," especially the "mother and child code," that leads him to make small objects characterized by a very simple and playful beauty, in a style reminiscent of children's toys.

Pino funnel. Alessi. 1998.

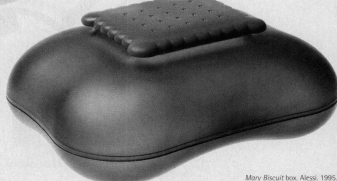

Mary Biscuit box. Alessi. 1995.

Mami saucepan. Alessi. 1999.

Nutcracker. Alessi. 1993.

Happy Species container/ sprinkler. Alessi. 1997.

Merdolino brush. Alessi. 1993.

Stefano Giovannoni **917**

Cleaning bucket. Alessi. 1993.

Lilliput condiment set. Alessi. 1993.

Fruit bowl. Alessi.

Axel Kufus

Born Essen, 1958. The designs of Axel Kufus are based on four premises: the creation of a modular system that is easy and cheap to produce, efficient storage in a small space, simple assemblage, and versatility in the arrangement of modules through a choice of combinations. It is a style in which functional considerations dictate the whole process, without any concessions to esthetics, and in which the object is defined by its own construction.

FNP. 1991.

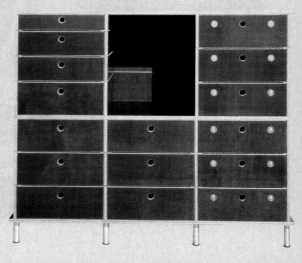

Lader. 1995.

Lader. 1995.

Eeva Kokkonen

Born 1959, Finland. Eeva Kokkonen is one of the prime movers of the innovative dynamism that has defined the latest trends in Finnish design. Her work springs from exhaustive experiments with traditional materials like wood and a simplification of manufacturing techniques. All her furniture is characterized by its austerity and high quality.

Freja. 1991.

Two Chairs, 1990.

Volkswagen, 1989.

Josef Frank

Born1885; died 1967. Josef Frank was an Austrian designer best remembered for his contribution to the conservative style, although when he moved to Sweden he came under the influence of the latest trends there. Frank's work is characterized by its eclecticism and functionalism; his outstanding designs include the *A81 IF* chair, from the early 1930s, and textiles such as *Mirakel*, from 1934.

Couch in black. Architects.

Armchair in leather. Architects.

White armchair. Architects.

Geerrit Thomas Rietveld

Born Utrecht, 1888; died 1964. The Dutch architect and decorator Geerrit Thomas Rietveld began his career as a cabinetmaker, but he soon changed course to become a member of De Stijl in 1919. He made an important contribution to the First Congress of Modern Architecture in 1928. Works such as the red and blue armchair, 1917, anticipated the new language that was to emerge for furniture design and interior decoration.

Wooden chair. Architects.

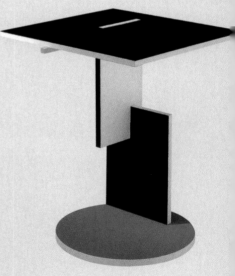

Lacquered table. Architects.

Red and blue armchair. Architects.

Herbert Ludwikowski

Herbert Ludwikowski defines the minimalist lines of his furniture as a natural reaction to the new technologies. His work is based on the principle of "less is more" espoused by the German architect Mies van der Rohe, and on the trust he places in natural lines and forms to fit into any setting. Many of his pieces are built on freestanding turning supports made of metal tubing, and are not supported by the wall.

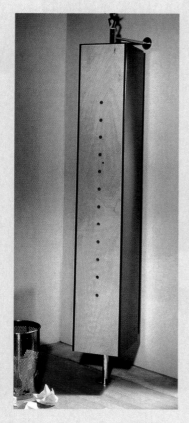

Calipso closet. 1994.

Calipso closet. 1994.

Tutto. 1989.

Tutto. 1989.

Laser. 1989.   *Taifun.* 1986.

Klaus Wettergren

Born Denmark, 1943. A Danish designer marked by the styles of the years 1930–1945, dominated by the use of natural woods like cherry and elm; an explicit exploration of craft techniques; and the use of sober, elegant, almost pompous forms that alternate curves and straight lines.

Meditation.

Lobby Chair.

President.

Poul Bjerregaard

Jebjerb, 1945, Dinamarca. Para este creador, el diseño de muebles es una labor de gran peso en el mundo de la arquitectura. Sus obras buscan satisfacer un propósito funcional y anhelan provocar un sugerente efecto visual. La apariencia escultórica, la ergonomía y el pleno confort definen cada una de las obras del creador danés.

Mesa extensible. 1990.

Sillón *Freja*. 1990.

Sunbed. 1990.

Holst Soren

Born 1947, Denmark. Holst Soren is one of the key figures in Danish design. His work is characterized by his clear desire to follow the rationalist premises that prevailed in the 1950s and 1960s. Functionality, compositional rigor, and limited production are the touchstones of his long professional career.

S.H. chair. 1991.

S.H. couch. 1991.

35° 16' dining room table.

André Ricard

Born Barcelona, 1929. André Ricard, the first president of the Spanish Designers' Association, has been an industrial designer since 1958, whilst also teaching and producing design theory, and his long career has included work for companies like Amat, Antonio Puig, Moulinex, and Tatay. His work generally focuses on everyday objects, and he follows each stage of the manufacturing process to ensure that the resulting products answer to criteria other than mere financial profit. Items such as the postbox created for Tatay in 1990, the Quorum range for Perfumes Puig from 1981, and the Olympic torch from 1990 are just some of the designs that have sealed Ricard's status as one of the most important of all Spanish designers.

Quorum range. 1981.

Postbox. 1990.

Tatú lamp. 1972.

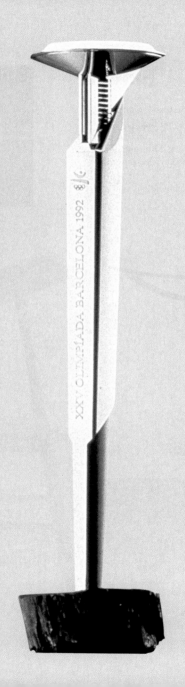

Olympic torch. 1990.

Oscar Tusquets

Born Barcelona, 1941. Oscar Tusquets studied in the Escuela de Artes y Oficios from 1955 to 1960. He is a founder member of Bd Ediciones de Diseño, a company for which he designs furniture and accessories. In 1983 he also began working for Italian firms, and made his mark as a creator of sculptural forms with daring combinations and a practical spirit.

Bìo Luz Lamps. 1985/1989.

Astrolabio. 1998. Driade.

Victoria. Driade. 1995.

Potro. 1990.

Gacela. 1991.

Tierra and *Luna* rugs, B.d., 1987.

Giorgio Manzali

Born Ferrara, 1941. Giorgio Manzali is a striking example of the confluence of different forms of expression in a single artist. His multidisciplinary work results in pieces with sculptural forms and warm colors, with sensual curves going in opposite directions but in perfect harmony. His design generally focuses on everyday requirements.

Charlie desk. 1990.

Rudy. 1990.

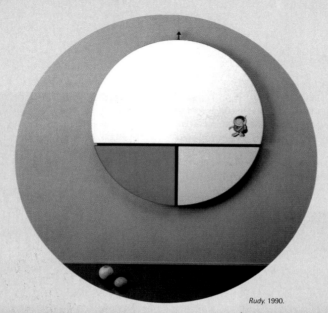

Rudy. 1990.

Gransera. 1990.

Konstantin Grcic

Born Munich, 1965. After working for a year in
Jasper Morrison's studio, Konstantin Grcic formed
his own company in 1991 to develop interior decoration and industrial design projects for companies
like Arteluce, Cappellinio, and Moormann. His work
is characterized by the use of very simple lines that
reveal the influence of the Nordic masters.

KGB, 1994.

Steep, 1995.

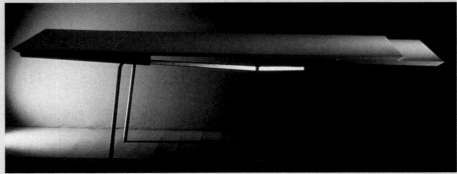

KGB, 1994.

Steep, 1995.

Kim Brun

Born Copenhagen, 1950. Kim Brun is one of the leading lights in new Danish design. His long training as a cabinetmaker gave him a theoretical grounding that he was later able to apply to his designs. His work is mainly inspired by tradition and draws on local landscapes and natural materials, especially different types of woods. Brun's main strength lies in his ability to reinterpret Scandinavian rationalism.

Chair, 1990.

Bookcase, 1990.

Armchair, 1989.

Armchair, 1990.

Kim Brun **947**

Pierangelo Caramia

Born Cisternino, 1957. Pierangelo Caramia, an Italian architect living in Paris and one-time associate of Philippe Starck, is a very cosmopolitan designer. His work has been marketed in Japan, France, and Italy through companies as prestigious as Cassina, Alessi, and Doublet. His objects reflect the close relationship between industry and craftsmanship in modern times, and constantly seek to enhance the quality of life of those who use them. He has also designed several outstanding interiors, such as the Bond Street Café in New York and La Pigalle in Paris.

Trevi. 1991.

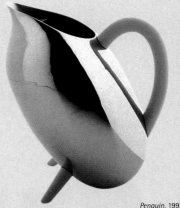

Penguin. 1993.

Tabula table and *Aura* chair. 1996.

Black Josephine, 1995.

Arild & Helge

Arild Aines and Helge Taraldsen formed their eponymous company in 1982, and they have gone on to supply the leading Norwegian design companies with a great many pieces that can be easily installed in any space. Their designs are also characterized by their comfort, ergonomic conception, and careful selection of materials marked by their smoothness, texture, and quality.

Rolls.

Focus 2.

Focus 1.

Josef Hoffmann

Born Pirnitz, 1870; died Vienna, 1956. The Austrian designer Josef Hoffmann founded the Vienna Secession, which rejected the styles of the past and the ornamental details based on nature that typified the Viennese Jugend style. Hoffmann, in contrast, sought inspiration in abstract geometrical forms, and these became the starting point for all his designs. He put these ideas into practice with cube-shape or elongated rectilinear pieces of furniture that were put on show in several Secessionist exhibitions. Many of his works, such as the *371* chair from 1906, incorporate small spheres that break up their straight lines.

Armchair. Architects.

Armchair. Architects.

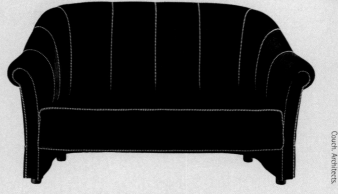

Couch. Architects.

Side tables. Architects.

Arnold Merckx

Born Netherlands, 1941. The ultimate goal of the designs of Arnold Merckx is the creation of objects that effortlessly fit into the various marketing strategies of the company for which he is working. This involves intensive research into the needs of the consumer. His esthetic approach is defined by the combination of basic geometrical forms, resulting in a typically Postmodern look dominated by simplicity and functionality.

Lady. 1991.

Lady. 1991.

Sfinx. 1989.

Sfinx. 1989.

Diabolo.

Giuseppe di Somma

The professional training of the Italian designer Giuseppe di Somma was complemented by studies in advertising and neoarchitecture. His works are characterized by their powerful visual impact, based on chromatic combinations and a bold linearity. His designs embrace a wide variety of forms and a minimalist touch.

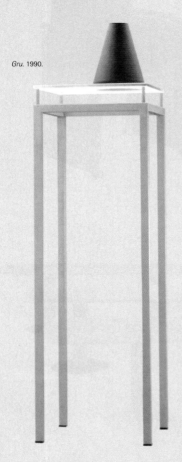

Gru. 1990.

Hans. 1991.

Step. 1990.

Trends

The enormous changes undergone in the modern world in the last few years have obviously had an impact on our lifestyle, not only in practical terms but also in esthetic ones, and we can now introduce into our homes decorative trends and styles that were unimaginable only a few years ago. These new tendencies include the assimilation of ecological concepts, of such relevance in other walks of life, into design; the borrowing of old designs, now considered classics, as elements in a new decoration, in accordance with the concept of cyclical fashions; the use of pieces of furniture as small-scale artworks or sculptures; the interpretation of foreign ideas and trends — be they oriental, ethnic, or native American — and their integration into our culture; playing with light; the inclusion of ceramic pieces as attractive complements; new furniture in inflatable plastic; and finally, the continuation, yet again, of the concepts of the minimalist movement — seen in furniture design with simple lines and forms.

Of all the sections that follow, that on ecological design is particularly noteworthy, due to its awareness of the environment. New uses assigned to old furniture; the recycling of chairs, lamps, and tables to adapt them to a more modern setting; and the restoration, polishing, and waxing of old desks and consoles are all evidence of a trend that is acquiring increasing popularity and opening up great possibilities in home decoration, as it is both functional and respectful of the environment.

The last chapter of this survey of international interior design in the last few years sets out merely to summarize, in graphic terms, some of those trends that, through their originality or exclusivity, are influencing present-day attitudes to the difficult task of furnishing up our homes.

Historic reruns

Set of two balls for tea with a support designed by Otto Riit Veger and Josep Knau, both members of the Bauhaus. 1924.

Some companies, such as Alessi in Italy, have produced limited editions of furniture and accessories that were landmarks in the history of modern design.

Sugar bowl and milk jug, with tray and tongs. Design by Marianne Brandt and Helmut Schulze. 1928.

Service for oil
and vinegar.
Design by
Christopher
Dresser. 1885.

Toast rack. Christopher
Dresser. 1878.

Cocktail shaker.
Anonymous.
Ca. 1925.

Table clock. Quartz movement.
Design by Pio Manzú. 1966.

Tea service with samovar. Design by
Eliel Saarinen. 1933–1934.

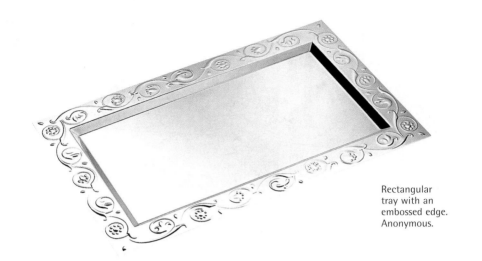

Rectangular tray with an embossed edge. Anonymous.

Tea and coffee service. Designed by Marianne Brandt. 1924.

Television made with compressed pieces of wood and glue without formaldehyde.

Table and chair made of plastic materials obtained from boxes of Maggi.

Stationery made with recycled paper.

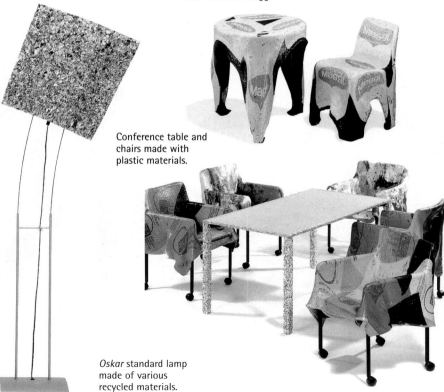

Conference table and chairs made with plastic materials.

Oskar standard lamp made of various recycled materials.

Small table obtained from the compression of plastic cups.

Ecological design

Modern design increasingly favors the rational use of biodegradable materials and waste to make furniture and other objects. Mussel shells, potato starch, and compressed pieces of wood can all provide alternatives to conventional materials that are intrinsically inconsiderate of the environment.

Pillars of light made from recycled plastics.

Bathroom sink made of recycled plastics.

Chairs made of recycled plastics.

Cutlery made of
potato starch.

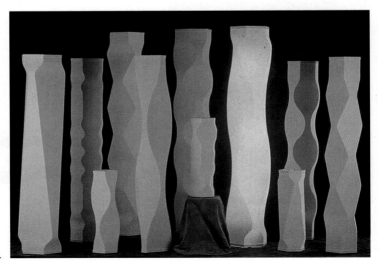

Lamps.

Furniture-sculpture

Today's designs of furniture and accessories
are not only aimed at mass production; there
is also a trend toward individual pieces,
unique objects lying somewhere between
sculpture and furniture.

Table. Design by Medina
Campeny. 1999.

Table. Design by Enric
Pladevall. 1999.

Container. Design by Josep
Montoya. 1999.

Table set. Design by Jonathan Daifuku. 1999.

Chair. Design by Beat Keller. 1999.

Chair form. Design by Manuel Alvarez. 1999.

The return of
the organic

Sensually shaped couches, the return of classic forms, simple lines, and eclecticism are some of the distinguishing traits of the new tendency toward organic furniture design. Monique and Sergio Savarese of Dialògica bring this trend to life by using the colors of the day – browns, ochers, and deep purples – and materials like maple, laminated steel, and dyed leather.

Verdulero. 1999.

Couch. 1999.

Cabinet Tyles. 1999.

Console. 1999.

Small table. 1999.

Couch. 1999.

Coordinated Design

Coordinated Design seeks to unify a space with interrelated furniture and accessories all within the same style. Michael Graves, for example, has collaborated with Dornbracht, Duravit, and Hoesch to come up with the Dreamscape line, an all-inclusive bathroom decoration that includes bathroom fittings, faucets, furniture, and accessories.

Free-standing bathtub.
Hoesch.

Dreamscape. 1999.

Bathroom fittings fixed
to the wall. Duravit.

Sink with fitted half-
pedestal. Duravit.

Raised
closet.
Duravit.

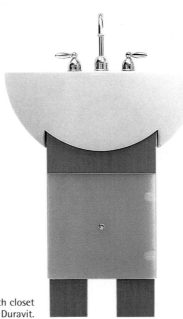

Sink with closet
incorporated. Duravit.

Double-handle faucet. Dornbracht.

Single-handle faucet. Dornbracht.

Wall faucet. Dornbracht.

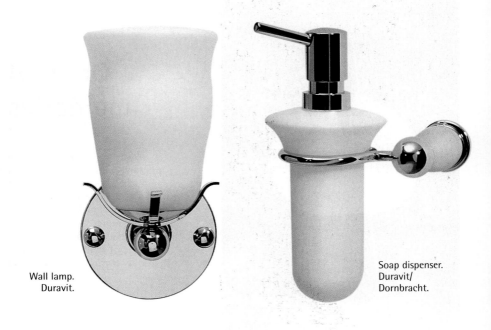

Wall lamp.
Duravit.

Soap dispenser.
Duravit/
Dornbracht.

Soap dish.
Duravit/Dornbracht.

Oriental memories

Western design is currently producing innumerable objects and pieces of furniture that reveal a strong oriental influence. The Mamo Nouchies collection, designed by Ingo Maurer, Mombach, and Noguchi, is a range of multicultural lamps inspired by the Japanese tradition of akari.

Poul Poul. 1999.

Samurai. 1999.

Mahbruky. 1999.

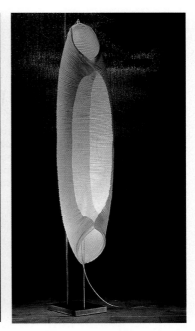

Babadul. 1999

Alodri. 1999.

Gaku. 1999.

Back to the forge

Josep Cerdá creates furniture and accessories by molding metals like iron and then decorating and painting them. He represents a trend that is increasingly popular in modern decoration, though its roots lie in the art of the medieval forges.

Detail of the console.

Console.

Hall table and
matching mirror.

Wadi-Musa.

Handle.

Handle.

The incorporation of metal structures in functional spaces helps add a modern touch.

The aluminum window panes and the metal frames of the furniture stand out in a setting lit by a large window.

Flashes of metal

Metal designs are extremely popular in present-day decoration. Stainless steel, aluminum, iron, and other metals, often combined with materials like wood, give an avant-garde look to any part of the house.

Easy chair with a frame in anodized aluminum. *Volare 986* model, designed by Jan Armgardt for Leolux.

Stainless steel bookcase.

Center table made of stainless steel, glass, and wood. *Volare 558* model, designed by Jan Armgardt for Leolux.

Simple forms and straight lines

The lines in modern bathrooms are moving toward an increasing simplification, reminiscent of Japanese tastes. Robust materials like woods specially treated against humidity and a predominance of stainless steel will be the distinguishing features in the coming years.

Alukit bathroom, designed by Mark Sandler. Boffi.

Sink, designed by Piero Lissoni. Boffi.

Minimal, designed
by Giulio
Gianturco. Boffi.

Punto bathroom,
designed by Luigi
Massoni. Boffi.

Gleams of light

The medieval tradition of stained-glass windows has made a comeback in contemporary decoration with designs reminiscent of Art Nouveau and Catalan Modernism. Teams of master craftsmen – such as the internationally renowned Artistas Vidrieros de Irún headed by José Luis Alonso – are producing leaded and painted windows in various styles, including Renaissance, Gothic, and Art Deco. Their intention is to restore the place of stained glass as an important decorative element in interior design.

Painted window. Artistas Vidrieros de Irún.

Skylight. The sunlight provides a multicolored effect. Artistas Vidrieros de Irún.

Renaissance stained-glass window. Artistas Vidrieros de Irún.

Partition with painted glass and leading. Artistas Vidrieros de Irún.

Ceramic art

The use of traditional Portuguese tiles is becoming more widespread in today's rustic-style decorations.

Mythical scene.

Martial motifs.

Altarpiece.

Figure from banquet.

Vase of flowers.

Art on the table

A combination of classic harmony and avant-garde style, with the addition of a few personal touches, marks the current trends in laying tables.

Lunch service.

Design by Paloma Picasso for Villeroy & Boch.

China by Christofle.

Coffee service
by Christofle.

Dinner service in bone
china from Villeroy &
Boch and Gallo.

China, glasses, and
cutlery from
Villeroy & Boch.

Au Coeur de la Foret from Sia Diseño.

Equilibre from Sia Diseño.

Millennium from Sia Diseño.

Chameleon objects

They look like pieces of furniture or accessories with a specific function, but they can be taken apart to convert into original gadgets. These works by the British designer Daniel Weil make innovative and surprising demands on both functionality and creativity.

H-Arp lamp.

Claire fruit bowl.

This multi-purpose extendable table designed by Daniel Will provides versatility for writing or dining alike. Drawers provide storage for either cutlery or stationery.

Table vase.

Rein entrance table.

Container table.

Integral design

There is a growing trend in interior design to turn to integral decoration with coordinated ranges of furniture and accessories that have their own collective personality. The work of Josep Montoya embodies this idea of unity so typical of modern design.

Center table.

Nightstand.

Bar unit with an intense granite top.

Dresser in maple and
caoba woods.

Sideboard.

Detail.

Couch. Ikea.

Mattress with
cover. Ikea.

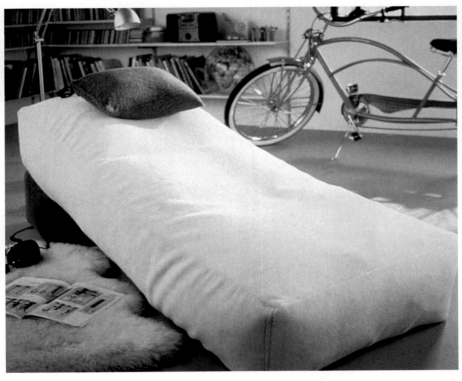

Inflatable furniture

Inflatable furniture is becoming increasingly common in modern decoration. The pieces hardly weigh anything, they are easy to maintain, and they effortlessly blend into any informal functional environment.

Armchair–pouf. Ikea.

Inflatable couch and pouf upholstered in denim.

Couch with cover.